# *I AM Presence*
# Diamond Heart Energy Workbook

with 12 MP3
Guided Activation Meditations

Rev. Brian T Roberts
*Minister of Light and Sound Healing*

AyniWrite Press
Albuquerque, NM

Copyright © 2016 by Brian T Roberts

Credit to Matt Sean Singer for engineering all music for the 12 Diamond Heart CD's/MP3's

Poetry by Brian T Roberts unless otherwise noted

All rights reserved. No part of this book may be reproduced or transmitted in any form or by any means without written permission of the author, except in the case of brief quotations embodied in critical reviews and certain other noncommercial uses permitted by copyright law. For permission requests, contact the author at www.LifeseedCodes.com.

AyniWrite Press, Albuquerque, NM
Printed in the United States of America

I AM Presence Diamond Heart Energy Activation Workbook / Brian Timothy Roberts
ISBN 978-0-9907550-8-1

# Within You

*The God Seed, the Sananda Codes, the Cosmic Christ Consciousness, the Buddha Nature is all a part of your present and future, your Diamond Heart, the Self.*

The Masters say there is nothing you can do to accelerate or even delay what is your unfolding in the Divine Plan. However you can make the journey more enlightening, creative, inspirational and satisfying for yourself by the focus of will, wonder and intent.

These meditations work. Feedback from users describe them as *"magical, creative and restorative"*.

The 12 minute *I AM* meditation is for <u>daily</u> invocation of the "Light", a must-do for spiritual travelers because of the astral shadow and dense energies of the planet.

The Heart Mantra at the end of the guided meditation drops you into your own heart chakra. Repeat the Bija mantra "*Hrim*" in your mind and then let it go. Visualize the color pink and then let that go. Sit in the silence for as long as you desire.

Please exit your meditations gracefully, easily and gently. You are working with powerful sub-atomic energies.

Three things to develop:

1. Keep your chakras aligned, cleared, open and balanced.
2. Live a cord-free life - free, that is, of people's energetic attachments.
3. Stay entity free.

Do ONE Activation per week . . . Repeat the one you are on every day if you like but stay to one unit per week. After you get to #8 you can use (#8) as frequently as you desire.

You have the workbook. Read it, share it. Invite a friend or family member to meditate with you.

Be sure to look at the special offer for a free Diamond Heart session with Brian at the end of this workbook. Also pick up the download instructions for receiving the important, free audio recordings of each meditation.

Blessings, *Brian Timothy Roberts*

---

## TO FULLY EXPERIENCE
### the twelve Diamond Heart activations, download and listen to the free audio recordings of the meditations

Sound vibration is one of the strongest ways to trigger activations so it is recommended that you listen to the mp3's for your activations and use this workbook as a secondary support.

### For instructions on how to get your
## FREE Diamond Heart Activation MP3's

go to page 105 of this workbook.

# Three Ways to do the Activations

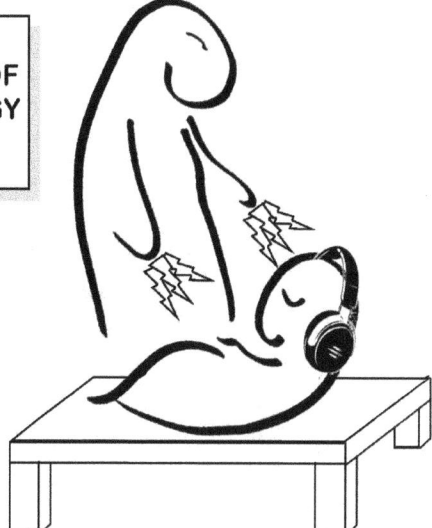

WHILE RECEIVING ANY OR ALL KINDS OF MASSAGE OR ENERGY BODYWORK

IN A GROUP

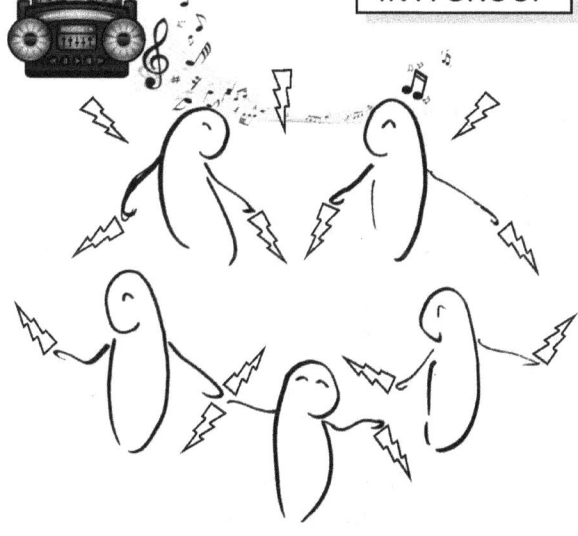

*THERE IS POWER IN GROUPS!*

SITTING IN THE LIGHT OF TRUE SELF

# The Door Bell

*The sacrament begins the moment the door bell rings
All around you are the guides, magic and colors
Invocation is a wondrous thing.
Secretly you have set your intention, without telling yourself,
or, even any of the others. Welcome!
As far as these times are concerned,
there are three proper modes of transportation,
at three speeds: a tourist bus, a local, and an express.
Mercy, Economy and the Daring not to go ahead of all the rest
are said in the Tao to be the Three Great Treasures.
From Mercy comes Understanding, Compassion and Love,
From Economy comes Generosity and Friendship.
Daring Not To Go ahead of others
brings out the deep and profound dimensions of a Solar leadership.
One inspired by the Sun,
One inspired by the Sun of Truth,
One inspired by the Sun of Beauty,
One inspired by the Sun of Essence,
One inspired by the Sun of Fulfillment,
One inspired by the Great Central Sun of the One.
The sacrament begins the moment the door bell rings.
All around you the guides, magic and colors.
Invocation is a wondrous thing
you have set your intention without telling yourself,
Or, even any of the others. Excellent!
Such a glorious game, such a gift from above.
Such a passionate play, such a way to discover.
Each step that we take, over this wholesome terrain,
We make a wish once more, for this soft gentle rain of love.
The song of the wind, to ease up the mind, and the time.
I Know we are all kingdom bound, I can see.
Bound to take our own sweet time, that is.
Happy travels, happy trails.
I'll be waiting for the door bell to ring.
Ready!
The sacrament begins the moment the door bell rings.
All around you the guides, magic and colors,
Invocation is a wondrous thing.
You have set your intention without telling yourself,
or even, any of the others.
Excellent! Ready! Welcome!*

# Table of Contents

Within You ..................................................................................................... iii

Three Ways to do the Activations ................................................................ v

The Doorbell .................................................................................................. vi

Preface ........................................................................................................... ix

Introduction to the Diamond Heart Energy 12 DNA Activations ............ xi

A Story: Zen Dragons, Snakes and Children ............................................. xiii

[1] Anchoring ................................................................................................ 1

[2] What DHEA IS and IS NOT .................................................................... 3

[3] Our Ceremony: The Invocations ............................................................ 5

    Diamond Heart Session Protocol ........................................................ 10

[4] The Twelve Activations: program descriptions and Meditations ..... 13

    **Step One: Body Elemental- Conscious Mind- Super Mind** .............. 15

        Affirmation : *I AM the Resurrection of my body/ mind/ spirit* ............ 15

        Meditation: On the Virtue of Alignment .......................................... 17

    **Step Two: Communication** .................................................................. 21

        Affirmation: *I AM Multidimensional communications* ..................... 21

        Meditation on the Virtue of Openness/Communication ................. 23

    **Step Three: Guidance and Intuition** .................................................. 29

        Affirmation: *I AM a Being Divinely Guided* ....................................... 29

        Meditation on the Virtue of Intuition ............................................... 31

    **Step Four: Co Creation, Talents, Productivity** .................................. 35

        Affirmation: *I AM a Magical being of Infinite Creativity* .................. 35

        Meditation on the Virtue of Co creation .......................................... 37

    **Step Five: Covenants, Purpose and Plan** .......................................... 41

        Affirmation: *I AM unfolding my Covenants with the Divine Plan* ... 41

        Meditation on the Virtue of Unity/ a Deep Oneness ...................... 43

    **Step Six: Organization and Co Operation** ........................................ 47

Affirmation: *I AM re-defining, re-developing, and re-directing my personal database to be in alignment with my higher self* ............................................... 47

Meditation on the Virtue of Momentum .......................................................... 49

### Step Seven: Synergy and Fluidity ...................................................................... 53

Affirmation: *I AM Up regulating and Up grading automatically* ............................ 53

Meditation on the Virtue of Beauty ................................................................. 55

### Step Eight: Self Maintenance, Filtration, Protection ..................................... 59

Affirmation: *I AM a Being of Violet Fire* ............................................................ 59

Meditation on the Virtue of Self Awareness ..................................................... 61

### Step Nine: Grounded in Awareness .................................................................. 65

Affirmation: *I AM the Balance and Harmony required* ........................................ 65

Meditation on the Virtue of a Resurrection ...................................................... 68

### Step Ten: Peace, Power, Prosperity ................................................................. 71

Affirmation: *I AM Manifesting what I need* ....................................................... 71

Meditation on the Virtue of Peace that Flows ................................................... 73

### Step Eleven: I Dream with Awareness .............................................................. 77

Affirmation: *I AM Awake in Life my Dreams I do recall* ...................................... 77

Meditation on the Virtue of Continuity ............................................................ 80

### Step Twelve: The Returning Point, The Octave, Angel Eyes ......................... 83

Affirmation: *I AM Accessing the Gifts of my Past with Guidance* ......................... 83

Meditation on the Virtue of Seeing with Angel Eyes .......................................... 87

**Poem:** Sun/Son/Daughter Illumination ....................................................................... 90

**Appendix i:** Affirmations List for the 12 DHEA ...................................................... 91

**Appendix ii:** Declaration of the Light ..................................................................... 92

**Appendix iii:** The Reset Exercise ............................................................................ 93

**Appendix iv:** Re-Set / Namáste Exercise ................................................................ 94

**Appendix v:** Standing Wave, Take 5 Re-Patterning Your Relationship with Gravity ...... 95

**Appendix vi:** Bija Seed Meditation ......................................................................... 97

**Appendix vii:** 'What DHEA is Not' Form .................................................................. 100

**Meet the Author** ............................................................................................... 103

**Free MP3 Download Information** ......................................................................... 106

# Preface

The most interesting thing about the Diamond Heart Energy Activation book and 12 MP3's is that meditation caused this to come into being. I did not start with any idea to create them. The guided meditations came first. Actually the energy was downloaded into me first.

I had not played the guitar really at all for 14 years. One of my mentors told me that If I wanted to know what was the best plan for my life—personally, professionally and spiritually—that I should do a twenty minute meditation for 21 days. I expected that a bolt of lightning with a "Dear Brian message" would drop into my living room, but no such thing. What happened was that after 21 days of intent and meditation, I started playing the guitar and chanting. At this same time I was taking trainings with new age teachers as was the case for me for many, many years. Seattle was a great place for me for this because great people came through here. I did an exercise in time travel and began studying some material from a book that I was going to do a training in. The training on the outer level never happened but internal energy really did happen.

My intent was to align and balance my Trinity of Mind-Body-Spirit or, to put it more precisely, to contact and align my guardian angel, my self and my body elemental. As a trained pendulum dowser, I used my LifeWeaving charts and divined that I needed to sit for twenty minutes to cause this alignment to happen. That first download was very powerful and I barely got off the couch the whole day. My percentage of integration was 100% at the end of the session. I continued for one week with this activation before moving on.

After this alignment, I began working with people in a very new and curious way using guided meditations, singing, and guitar and bodywork. Eventually I had the outline for the 12 unique sessions. I would do a session with people and they would ask me if they could book a session right then and there but I always requested that they take a period of integration before setting up any follow-up sessions. I did not really want to generate a practice. I did not want to generate any dependency on myself. In fact I had to write a form of an agreement with people which is in the book called "What the Diamond Heart Energy Activations are NOT". Source energy never forces it self upon anyone. Pure heart energy has no agenda but to shine. I was Self initiating and I AM sharing this very pure process because I had the great good fortune to have so many great mentors from so many rich traditions over many, many years.

After finishing the book a client told me to record the sessions onto a CD so people could have access to the energy/material. I thought the idea was absolutely crazy even though in the meantime I am writing and recording with a great vitality. I did have a picture that I generated from my computer showing before and after an activation. It was amazing—the room turned Archangel Michael blue. The whole energy changes when you invoke a higher power, *amen, alleluia, namáste*. So we did it. We put the material, the intent, the 12 minute I AM meditation, the Invocations and music for the download meditation on a CD and sat together and did it. Wow was that cool. It worked . . .

What was really beautiful at this point was that I was hands free to be doing energy work, bodywork, healing while the guided meditation was playing.

What was even more beautiful was that every one that completed the work went on to demonstrate some exquisite new talent and ability. Artists began to blossom. Sales people got new territory and big checks. People got out of bad relationships and into really great ones, myself included. There is magic in that *I AM* Presence and that is true for everyone.

I believe that because of my background in healing and meditation (I have performed over a thousand ceremonies, hypnotherapy and Alpha Brain Balancing) of course my art is going to be colored by these. But somebody else can make the same discovery and communicate it in their own unique way. Anyone who is empowered by the Diamond Heart is FREE to utilize all of it and any of it freely and joyfully. It is Universal. It is Pure and it is Self designed by Your Self, not mine. I have provided the template. You can provide the energy and intent to re-direct new and exciting ways to bring about a higher self awareness and fulfillment for yourself and the world around you.

If you do get into the Diamond Heart please feel free to go on [LifeSeedCodes.com](LifeSeedCodes.com) and download some of the FREE music. If you feel you need some support than I am more than happy to assist you, to clear you and provide feedback to you on how you might deepen your appreciation of it.

Months and years later I will talk with people who got activated and they will share with me many great and exciting things that are happening for them now in their lives. All great things happen to those who love. All great things happen to those who contact the real self.

Blessing on the Journey,

Brian

# Introduction to the Diamond Heart Energy 12 DNA Activations

DNA Activation is a term developed by modern healers, energy workers and quantum wellness facilitators to describe a process that focuses on up-grading, up-lifting and up-regulating the energy holding, or working capacity, within the human energy field. A simple example of a light bulb will be sufficient to appreciate—that a 220-watt bulb will offer more illumination than a 20-watt bulb. What is exposed in this illumination, is the tremendous range and capacity of the human being that is in the latent state. The activations gather more energy/light.

The use of mechanisms and tools such as invocations, focused intent, breath, visualization, causal body/etheric body downloads, and sound vibrational healing results in the raising of atomic electro-magnetic energy that affects chakras, subtle energy, meridians and brain/body balance. This will result in higher levels of performance in all human endeavors.

The Diamond Heart Energy Activations and all music were synthesized, composed, written and developed by Brian Roberts—but not without many years of study, meditation and apprenticeship with New Age or modern initiates, quantum healers and spiritual masters. The series of 12 sessions—generally 60 minutes in length—forms the foundation for the work and will be listed below. Although it is best to be in the company of a facilitator, MP3's are also available! One to two week intervals between each step is optimal. If you own the MP3's you can use them daily. Also, Track 2 of the 12 minute *I AM Meditation* is recommended for daily use. The track can be downloaded for free at www.LifeSeedCodes.com.

Focus, commitment and dedication play a role as well, as part of the progress of human nature. Invocations are mental/emotional statements that we offer up to the superconscious mind, or higher self, to activate or facilitate a flow of energy/information that transcends limitations and often renders the often impossible, possible. They are quantum mental/verbal instruments of peace, power and precision.

Session Template:

(1) Step or Program descriptions        12 Minutes
(2) The *I AM* Meditation               12 Minutes
(3) The Diamond Heart Invocations        9 Minutes
(4) The Download Meditation with Music  12 to 15 Minutes.

Note that each MP3 features a new presentation of original music by Brian Roberts

(5) Closing Benediction

The affirmations define the intent and character of each of the sessions. The energy for each session is a causal/etheric energy template that activates the individuals requesting an activation. In essence it is a baptism of Sacred Fire from the octave of love, the octave above. The discipline of spiritual unfolding is the directing of Intention, the receptivity of *allowing* and the appreciation of *grace*.

Please be sure to resource the additional Diamond Heart information found on the website www.LifeseedCodes.com. This includes the following:

- Introduction to the Diamond Heart—eight page essay
- Bija Seed meditation used for personal or group initiation. You can also receive it from Brian over the telephone
- Diamond Heart affirmations used on the twelve DHEA MP3's
- *The I AM* Meditation and other music, also available for free download.

# A Story:
# Zen Dragons, Snakes and Children

The old Zen monk had three treasures which he wove into all his lessons, lectures and teaching stories. Honesty was his first treasure, the honesty of Self-Examination and Self-Inquiry. Look into your light, see and notice your shadow. His second treasure was Clarity. He said, "Look and just see what truly is present. Do nothing to disturb the balance of things. Look, and you will see the balance through Clarity". His third treasure was Ceremony but others also called this going into the great silence or deep, deep meditation into boundlessness. "If you will let me teach you how to look, you will be free to see the existence, without prejudice, for yourself." He was radiantly compassionate.

When you discover what you are truly made of, there will be cause for great hearted joy.

The Master was lecturing to some monks one day and told them that, to become enlightened, one must first completely dis-arm himself and stand naked in front of a fire breathing dragon, free of all fear and projections. He loved to get the students attention this way. Do you understand what he asked his class? He was referencing one's shadow self. A student up front smiled and relaxed, and the Master locked eyes with him.

One of the new students in the back started laughing out loud. He knew there was no such thing as a dragon so he decided to play along with the master. He said "O.K. Master, *I AM* ready but will you please tell me how to find one, a dragon I mean". The master told him to listen carefully and he would be able to hear one as a dragon had been just speaking right through him. Everyone laughed out loud. The teacher loved the laughter and often said this opens the heart and mind for the Heart and Mind of Zen to enter. The new student sat very low and almost disappeared in the group.

They went on to talk about the story of the snake and the rope and, of course, everyone laughed out loud when the Master said that once you discover that the snake is really only a rope it does not matter how big the rope is, was, or will be. A rope is a rope is a rope like a mind is a mind is a mind. Get over it! The pesky petty little mind... go...

"One more story", he said affectionately to the students, "before we move along for the day". He smiled and said, there is a beautiful story which is purely fiction, about a Buddhist monk who heard about a group of travelers who had been stranded on a snowy mountain pass. Due to injury and very bad weather some in the party had been unable to get down the mountain; winter was a factor. A women, a Taoist nun who had fallen and broken a bone, was amongst them. This single monk, carrying provisions, herbs, kindling, tonics and blankets, went out to try to save whomever he could .

When the monk finally found the group, all but the Taoist nun were frozen to death. The nun was almost gone. The monk found a cave and was able to start a fire. He laid down his blankets but knew this would not be enough. He finally wrapped himself up with the woman, embracing her with great compassion and care; he called out to celestial forces attempting to "give her life", to place his body heat into this women. Outside a snow storm was raging. As the monk began chanting *"Om Mane Padme Hum"*, *"Om Mani Padme Hum"*, *"Om Mani Padme Hum"*, they fell into a deep trance of healing. A magical and increasingly brighter light, began to emanate from somewhere within the cave, eventually engulfing them both. They fell into a deep delicious sleep full of dreams, of songs, of chanting, of holy mantras, of visitations with divine and cosmic beings, of Shambala and Shangri-la. They were carried far away in Spirit!

They slept deeply and without interruption through the winter like two bears in hibernation. Spring came and finally they were able to arise and face the day, the weather and the spring. It was exactly as if, by some hidden command, that they arose and quietly readied themselves, a warm smile on each of their faces as they gestured with hands folded upon the heart, a namáste, a bow, a blessing. They ventured silently down the mountain and, when they arrived at a small village just after dusk, were immediately taken into great care and all of their needs were met. The next morning at sunrise a child, a son, was born to this couple. This women had given birth, miraculously. When the monk spoke to some of the village folk they gave him the good news. It is a boy, they said, and as beautiful as a Buddha.

One man told a story of a friend, a monk who had gone up the mountain but had perished in the storm. He no longer recognized this monk, his friend, as the monk had become totally transformed, radiant, luminous with light. He has crossed over, and yet, remained.

A double rainbow had appeared at the moment of birth and two golden eagles flew over the village. The child was able to speak within a few hours of birth, and later that day took a few steps. The village people believed that the nun was a queen, a goddess of some kind, as her beauty was radiant beyond description. The child, they thought, was a Buddha or a reincarnation of one very high Lama at least. His emanations were most auspicious and light.

The parents (the monk and former nun), the villagers thought, were some great masters of a long forgotten tradition, probably driven out by some gang or corrupted government. They were offered asylum in this valley and it was upon that Holy ground the child, called Zen, was born. Zen, the offspring of the union between Buddhism and Taoism.

A holy temple was erected on this site, and above the main doors it reads "Always be ready to completely abandon what you THINK may be sacred to you; to actually give birth to the Real and Divine in you, through you and all around you".

A long, long line of illustrious, illumined beings still flow out of this place and some summers, some leave the safety of this village and venture out over the mountain pass.

"Look, listen. One may come along this way here any day", said the Master.

# [1]
# Anchoring

*We live in a Universe of Ask, Seek And Knock.*
*We live in an Archangel Michael Universe.*
*We live in a Universe of Cause and Effect.*
*You have asked for the opportunity to come here and master this dimension.*
*You are the master of your destiny.*
*You only get to take the love you make.*
*You are here to master all the signs and the races*
*The steeper the hills, the greater the thrills.*
*Whatever you give you keep, and whatever you take you lose.*
*It is all done here with mirrors.*

Every day that I initiate a Diamond Heart Energy Activation, I touch into a fabric of reality that makes other best days seem dull by comparison.

I never could have climbed this mountain without my guides, physical and non-physical.

The greatest gift I believe that one man can do for another is to truly guide them to the Self and to the mansion of the Father's house, for freedom, for purpose and love.

This is NOT an attempt to create any Entity, Group, or Organization to dispense these activations, but rather, an effort to unveil to each individual the beauty and boundlessness of their own nature, and of the One Spirit, that is one's natural inheritance.

The I AM Presence of YOUR BEING runs the operations of the activations in ways that are simply too profound to define. Let the mystery unravel YOU to YOU for YOU within YOU.

*Ask.   Seek.   Knock.*
*And the door shall be opened to you.*
*Become an Anchoring Diamond.*

*Be a Part of a Wave of Wonder, Magic and Possibility:*
*The Diamond Heart Energy Activations*

It's a very simple process now that we have spent years fine tuning it. After a few sessions, I remember wondering "How could <u>one</u> ever teach the process?" Because we were so altered by the download, there was no way one could do more than two sessions in a day. One is plenty. So much light and so much energy. The sessions often took about four hours. Preparation, explanations, meditation and time for integration, the energy was so HIGH no one wanted to leave.

The process with synthesizing activations was running a parallel path to my music. After recording the Moola Mantra CD, I decided to use the background music for an *I AM* meditation CD and give it to clients to use in between sessions. We all liked it so much, we started using it in the DHEA sessions. I will often do Life Seed Energy Work, a subtle energy work, during this part of the session. Encouraging a friend to think about doing and sharing the sessions, she told me very enthusiastically to record the whole thing. She said that I held the sound/wave keys for these activations. I resisted for probably six months. When we finished the first Activation CD and listened to it together, a whole new world of possibilities was being opened. It went well beyond all expectations.

Now, this can be our journey together, a journey in the Diamond Heart, and a journey that can open you to a new and exciting level of unfolding and light, and you can use the activations to share with friends, clients and family! Doing the sessions is the best way to continue unfolding in the *I AM*. The goal is to use the CD's or MP3's until you no longer need them and can truly hold the energy for a group. Also, you might just find that you simply want to focus on your own living, loving and learning process with your own *I AM* Presence, and do the work here, while it is vibrating possibility for you! Your Intentions will make magic happen.

The Heart mantra on the end of the *I AM* Meditation Track 3, is a Bija Seed mantra from the holy tradition of the Vedas, and *I AM* happy to initiate anyone who wishes, over the telephone. The telephone is quite a reasonable medium for this; and while the TM people charge thousands, I simply ask for a donation.

The program descriptions that appear in the workbook and that are read on of each of the MP3's, can really hardly do justice to all that is involved. But it gives the conscious process some reference point. Although I am not usually very visual, I saw the descent of the guardian spirit/angel in a session #1 that I did with a woman in her 70's. Weeks later I saw her out shopping and she reported she was doing great and that she felt like she had a hat on for a few days after the sessions. Her crown chakra was lit up!

Read the program descriptions and especially the meditations as you work with the MP3's. You will get more out of the whole process. Also if you feel inclined to work with a group to share the excitement please do, <u>but do not copy the music.</u> The price is absolutely very reasonable and more can be purchased from me.

Blessings/Brian.

# [2]
# What DHEA *Is* and *Is Not*

## What DHEA *Is* NOT

What is clear to me, after the practice of energy work and meditation for many years, is that one is constantly in a more focused state of self-discovery and creativity. It is important when considering participating in the Diamond Heart research and guided meditations, that one understands what these activations are **NOT.**

1. *This is not* a form of therapy, or hypnosis of any kind or persuasion.
2. *This is not* a religious belief program.
3. *This is not* the practice of medicine, diagnosis or mental health assessment.
4. *There are no* beliefs required outside a normal trust that one is connected to a Universal power

that created us and maintains us, and that we are connected to this source of power through grace. Your sovereignty is held as a sacred trust.

5. *Participants are free to stop this inquiry* at any time either during a session or after any session. Participation is totally voluntary. Each session is scheduled as desired.

6. *There are NO* suggestions or advice given concerning one's way of living, one's relationships and affiliations in any way that may be considered directives.

7. *There is never* any recruiting to join any organization, group or congregation.

# What DHEA *IS*

**What Diamond Heart Energy Activations are**, are the free use of our God-given attention and inquiry. This does not use any mechanical, electrical, or chemical means in our own body/mind/spirit. The sole purpose is for expanding our awareness and appreciation for the gifts *within*, both activated and utilized, and those we wish to awaken from a latent state. Also upon discovery, we acknowledge the free right of participants to share freely any and all of the discoveries obtained within, in any way that the individual may so choose. No secret hand shakes.

The Diamond Heart Energy Activations are quantum energy conversations that honor the giver and the receiver as equal partners in a journey of self-exploration. These sessions encourage a new and mature way of human interaction that acknowledges the sovereignty of each individual, their right to choose, and to make discovery that will enhance the human experience by directly bringing in more quantum, electro-magnetic energy.

It is therefore the responsibility of participants to determine if this is the appropriate time for such an adventure and to consider personally all things appropriate to such an exercise. The one absolute is to rest easy for a few hours afterwards and to consume sufficient amounts of water. (Rest easy means to lie down for at least one hour.)

I have read the statement and freely subscribe my signature. (*Optional*)

Name: _____

It is a good idea to keep a release form like this one around for safe keeping.

A clean copy is available in Appendix VII.

# [3]
# Our Ceremony
# The Invocations

## *I AM Presence Invocation*

*Beloved I AM Presence, what you mean to me,
I call upon you to help set me Free.
To guide, protect me and please lead the way
to the promised land, to those sparkling sands,
to the waters that flow out of the One true well of
that "I AM That I AM".*

*I AM a child of THAT One true One.
I AM a particle of THAT One True Sun.
I AM a song from THAT One True sound.
To This Limitless light I AM Heart-fully bound.*

*I AM a traveler on the sands of time.
Born of the essence of THAT One true Mind.
Your Love is my essence and Peace is my way.
Yesterday is a memory - I AM Present today.
To build in my experience, a master's touch,
That each passing day may
be golden as such.*

*That with each mountain you send for me to climb
I will grow closer to understanding your ways and mine.
That each bridge I cross over waters so deep,
I stay ever present in meditation, dreaming and sleep.
That each waking moment be real, open and ever new,
That each step I take brings me closer to you.*

*We call you the Diamond Heart because of our great love,
acknowledged that this is your gift showered to us from above.
I AM only as you created me to be.
I AM totally surrendered to thee.
Oh, I AM THAT I AM,
With love, for love, in love, as love.*

## The White Light Tube of Protection and Presence

*Beloved Mighty I AM Presence,
Light me and enfold me in my mighty, magic, electronic
TUBE of Ascended Masters' Light substance.
Make it so powerful that no human creation can pass through!
Please see that it keeps me Invulnerable, Invisible and Invincible
to everything but those energies that align
with my ascension into the Light.*

(Visualize This)

## The Wall of Blue Flame and Archangel Michael's Sword

*Beloved Mighty I AM Presence keep me surrounded with a wall of
Blue Flame for added protection outside my Tube of Light.
I call upon Archangel Michael and his legions of angels that support
to cut all cords that attach to me (us) in any way.
Cut us Free - Cut us Free - Cut us Free -
Cut us Free - Cut us Free - Cut us Free -
Cut us Free - Cut us Free - Cut us Free
Protect us until we are totally free in the Ascension into Light.*

# The Violet Flame of Unconditional Love and Transmutation

*Beloved I AM Presence, blaze through me now,*
*Your mighty, Violet, Consuming Flame of Unconditional LOVE.*
*Let me feel and absorb this energy, which far exceeds anything of human origin.*
*The Blue flame of the Father and the Pink flame of the Mother*
*combine to give energy, life and substance to the Violet Flame,*
*The purifying power of Divine love, which is the most powerful*
*and dynamic activity presently available to humanity.*

(Feel This)

*We focus now on the power of transmutation*
*and we request of the Violet flame to consume cause, effect, records,*
*And memory of those negative concepts, desires and feelings*
*in our beings and world that we are able to release at this time.*
*Replace this with as much light, love, purity and purpose*
*as we are able to percolate, sustain, radiate and maintain.*
*We actively invoke the Ascended Masters' electronic substance of light*
*from the octave above, from the octave of love.*

*I AM the Ascension into Light*

*I AM the Presence raising the atomic structure of the body*
*into full Illumination and Liberation.*

- Now visualize that the whole body has turned to crystalline substance.

- Visualize the Star of David, the six-pointed star at the forehead and, upon establishing contact with the Star, send this down into the very center of the Earth, into the healing temple in the center of the Earth. Request with your mind, *"Mother Earth receive my energy"* and immediately an impulse returns to us. And Mother Earth downloads into our spiritual matrixes, the LIFE SEED CODES necessary for upgrading and aligning with the morphogenic field of intelligence. Your magnetic field becomes charged. Now bring the Star back to reside in the heart. Take a nice, full breath and begin integrating.

- Now send the Star out through the crown chakra, out into the Sun and through, into the Great Central Sun; into the heart of the Father, and upon arrival, request of the Father, *"to receive our energies*". Immediately an impulse returns to us and we receive the LIFE SEED CODES to up-grade and up-regulate our life force intelligence. Gratefully acknowledge the gift and flow the Star back into your energy field residing at the heart. Again, breathe and Integrate. Your electronic substance is now charged.

(The following should be used in the long form or may be used as a short form for instant protection many times daily; memorize).

*I AM protected in my magic tube of White Light Ascended Master's energy*
*I AM protected by a wall of Blue Flame and Archangel Michael's*
*Legion of Light*
*I AM a Being of Violet Fire*
*I AM the Purity God Desires*
*I AM Star breathing Life Seed Codes of Father/Mother Ascension Essences*

(Bija Mantra Meditation)

Note that when you offer guided meditation and prayer, combine elements of structure and essence. Know where you are going and what you want to reinforce such as protection, clearing and making contact with the beloved *I AM* Presence. Then, speak your personal or group prayers, petitions and gratitude to God, the collective *I AM* Presence of angels and guides.

## The Great Invocation

*From the Point of Light within the mind of God,*
*Let light pour forth into the minds of men.*
*Let Light descend on Earth.*

*From the Point of Love within the heart of God,*
*Let Love pour forth from the heart of God*
*and may the Christ return to Earth.*
*May the Christ Consciousness prevail.*

*From the Center where the will of God is known,*
*Let purpose guide the little wills of men,*
*The purpose which the masters know and serve.*

*From the Center, which we call the race of men,*
*Let the plan of Love and Light work out and may it*
*seal the door to the darkness.*
*Let Love and Light and Power,*
*Restore the plan on Earth.*

(Please research this prayer and find out where it came from and how it is being utilized today. You will notice that persons of many different traditions—including healers, shamans and kahunas—are utilizing it.)

# Diamond Heart Session Protocol

## Diamond Heart Energy Activation Invocation

*Out of the fullness of the radiant life, we respectfully acknowledge our source and sustenance, our light and love, our supply and inspiration.*

*Thou Mighty Infinite Presence, All Pervading Intelligence, All Pervading Substance of Light, Thou Omni-Present, Omni-Potent, Omniscient ONE, we give praise and thanks unto the light, unto thee. We give praise and thanks unto the great Central Sun from whose rays we receive our light today.*

*We give our gratitude to you oh Mighty I AM that I AM and to all your Legions of Light and through your emissaries of Cosmic beings, Elohim, archangels and angels, the Ascended Masters, the Buddha's, the Christ's, the Avatars whom work tirelessly on behalf of humanity for it's Ascension into the light.*

*We salute the Collective I AM Presence and attune our life force energies with these benefic spirits, the Masters that do thy bidding to Up-Grade and Up-Regulate the electronic substance/bodies and activate the appropriate programs and life centers in the etheric and causal bodies and the DNA sequence for our initiations.*

*We acknowledge our own Holy I AM Presence and engage the sacred Fire with the utmost respect and admiration.*

*We affirm the direction and utilization of our new and unfolding abilities to* the service of humanity and transformation into light, into law and into love!

*So be it!*

(Ask out loud for the activation here or read the program description if desired.)

## The Activation Invocation

*In the Divine name of God, in the company of the Collective I AM, in the Presence of our Masters in Spirit I call forth the energies necessary to activate this Essential Program #_____ (say the number you are on and the affirmation associated with this session) for _____ (say the name of the person).*

*I Invoke all aspects of Divinity for all present.*

*I Invoke the White Fire Being.*

*I Invoke the Solar Causal Being.*

*I Invoke the I AM Presence.*

*I Invoke the Christ Presence, my holy mediator.*

*I Invoke my Body Elemental.*

*I Invoke my Guardian Angel.*

*I ask that the Essential Program # _____ be downloaded for _____ (client and practitioner) according to his/her highest good and for the harmony of Being, Purpose and Alignment of the Divine plan.*

*Beloved I AM Presence, download now, the program for Activation of the DNA and Essential Programs that allow for the harmonious upgrading and awakening of the Essential Energies within the Centers which interface the etheric and causal bodies.*

## Completion

This activation has now been successfully facilitated and will continue to integrate over the next few hours and days. The *I AM* presence now scans through my/our body/minds and clears all circuits and all space allowing for the fullest possible integration. We call upon the Violet Flame of Transformation for ourselves and all people we come into contact with this day to blaze into every electron of our life force and transform every life energy that we have ever mis-qualified. Consume or clear all effects, records and memory so that this activation will integrate and fully function.

*Beloved I AM Presence, please search through all areas of our being and bodies and delete anything that conflicts with these programs in any way shape or form.*

## Closing or Benediction

*Wondrous Presence Of the "Great I AM",*

*We give praise and thanks for this feeling of the certainty of thy presence,*

*growing and unfolding us.*

*We give all thanks for the support of those wonderful radiant beings*

*that do support us from the unseen world,*

*The great collective I AM Presence of Masters,*

*Angels,*

*Elementals,*

*and the Cosmic Beings.*

# [4]
# The Twelve Activations
# Program Descriptions & Meditations

Diamond Heart Energy Activations
STEP 1: DNA Essential Program Downloads

# Body Elemental • Body Awareness
# Body Intuition • Alignment of the Trinity

AFFIRMATION:
*I Am the Resurrection and the Life
of my Body/Mind/Spirit*

ESSENTIAL PROGRAM #1 DESCRIPTION:

This activation works with the alignment of the Body Elemental, the outer individualized Self and the Higher Self. This session sets the intention for a greater level of sensitivity to unfold with the physical body allowing one to hear, feel and intuit the body and all its needs. Each person is their own unique event and must march to the beat of their own inner self with attention on the elemental and guardian or higher self. The degree of unity, balance and cooperation determines the degree of mastery.

This program will allow you to intuit more accurately what nutrition is necessary for you at a given time as well as other healing modalities such as massage, rest, meditation and any other number of things that are relevant to your personal life.

It is important to add here that it is necessary to begin speaking to and reflecting upon the body with a new outlook. The Body Elemental is handling all the processes of running trillions of operations in the brain and central nervous system, in the glands of internal and external secretion, tissue regeneration and on and on. Yes, it is much too much for the conscious mind to fathom.

When man descended through the Seven Spheres and into the Earth and corresponding evolving aspects, he was given by The Creator, a Guardian Angel and a physical mentor in the form of the Body Elemental. This aspect is so invisible that in almost all cultures, it is simply overlooked and taken for granted, perhaps much like the Guardian Angel.

So this trinity of Body Elemental, Individual Ego and Higher Self—each with their own internal trinities—are brought into harmony through INTENTION, invocation and this Essential Program Download Activation. It may be noted that the individual is shaped by the Body Elemental, and not so much by his or her environment.

The Trinity of the higher self may be viewed as the "*I AM* Presence," the Christ presence and the individual spirit or entity whose home is the heart and the attendant three-fold flame. The Presence can never see anything of lack, limitation or disharmony and so the Christ Self, through the energy field, interfaces the individual aspect that evolves in the body with care, patience.

The Body Elemental has no recourse but to serve the master, the evolving spirit and this alliance, for the purpose of its own evolution. It is therefore suggested that one make a sign of appreciation, inwardly, to the Body Elemental for its support. Take a Moment! Take and send a breath of gratitude to our friend—our Body Elemental!

Take a Moment! Take and send a breath of gratitude to our friend—our Higher Self!

Listen and acknowledge the truth about yourself.

(Read the following affirmations to yourself in the first person.)

## Affirmations

*I AM a being of Sacred Fire.*

*I AM the Purity God desires.*

*I AM the Balance of Body, Mind and Spirit.*

*I AM the Breath of the Living Pulsating Light.*

*I AM a Thinker of whole, full and complete thought.*

*I AM a Feeler of regenerating joy and peace.*

*I AM an Atom of Divinity circulating in Space.*

*I AM a Traveler on the Master Path.*

*I AM a Flame of Wisdom, Love and Power.*

*I AM calling forth from my undivided Self, all that is necessary to succeed on all levels of being and transmitting this to the world.*

*I AM a Lover of Living; passionate and prepared to embrace truth and all the discoveries of my inheritance.*

*I AM today committing to a new and ever expanding field of possibilities.*

*I AM affirming the trinity of being, the Super-consciousness above and a sub-conscious appealing with love, and a Conscious mind—here and now present.*

*I AM the Resurrection and the Life of my Body/Mind/Spirit*

## Meditation

The *I AM* meditation on Track 2 of Activation #1 MP3 follows here.

## Meditations on the Virtues of the Diamond Heart

## #1

# Alignment
# Alignment of the Trinity

Affirmations: *I Am the Resurrection and the Life of my Body/Mind/Spirit*
*All the Power that ever was or will be is here now.*

The goal of these essays is not to try to jump over or supercede the great considerations of Aristotle, St Paul, or the Buddha on the necessity of developing human/divine qualities and virtue, but rather to see how these considerations may become more deeply rooted as we open our SELF to Grace, to ceremony, to activation and integration.

### *I AM That I AM I AM That I AM I AM That I AM*

*Nothing Exists but the great One, the All*
*Is calling each cell/self back from the far and removed.*
*A wide winged wind of gentle embrace*
*Circles around you and wishes to prove.*
*That this light that you sit in the vicinity of*
*Wants to yield to you, the seed of, the Divinity of Love*
*And the heart of belonging*

*I AM That I AM I AM That I AM I AM That I AM*

*When everything you once believed to be true,*
*Touches the garment of unveiled golden white hues,*
*Beyond the I, beyond mind, beyond the oceans too,*
*The hide and seek that you always play*
*Gives way to a sound too trumpeting to hush.*

*From feet to fingers one feels a familiar sacred rush,*
*of being born or of giving birth.*
*I AM That I AM I AM That I AM I AM That I AM*

*And for just a split second it rings.*
*And oh for the heart such solace it gives.*
*One micro second of a shattering bliss.*
*One sacred moment of a towering kiss.*
*One pause in silence's wanderings twists.*
*One fresh new revelation*
*That I AM*
*and simply Exist.*

*I AM That I AM I AM That I AM I AM That I AM*

# Alignment is our first Virtue

It is the recognition of our total dependence on the all that is. Lots of people think they have the luxury of a free will and lots of ego trying to prove this, to prove that, do this and do that! One day God was talking to a group of scientists and playing the creation game. Everything that God made, the scientists quickly followed successfully. Then God created an amazing Being of Light and Crystal, with wings and wands and wonder. *"Can you do this?"* asked the creator? One of the scientists leaned over and picked up some dust and then God said, *"Oh please use your own dust"*. You can co-create but creation, that is another story.

Alignment is the first step and it is a triple action of Courage, Confidence and Surrender. It is the kaleidoscope combination of color, and it transports one to a place of wonder, excitement and relationship. I exist and so does all of this. I did not create myself, so I must be connected to this all that is. Life is an interdependent arising and there is virtue in wholeness, my alignment and my alignment with life. I stand up, I open up and I face True North. All that is in me as expression, as possibility, as yet to be discovered me, comes to the peace of unity, organicity, surrender and realignment.

It is a blessing thing, a humbling thing, a surrendering thing and an empowering thing. I exist. *I AM*, but really only, *i am*. I am a child within these walls of electrons, protons and sub-atomic particles. Therefore, let not my beliefs be the thief's that steal away my alignment, but rather let me have the Courage and Confidence to surrender to this, to that which is beyond all speculation. Let me align, co-create and discover first what *I AM* made of. Then the door that no man can shut, and no man can open save Grace, will open. Alignment is for wonder and co-creation. Alignment is for self-discovery. Alignment is for beauty and balance and wholeness.

*Alignment happens and there is Virtue in Alignment*

*Alignment happens and there is Alignment in Virtue*

*Alignment is Virtue happening as Alignment*

*Alignment has wholeness as Virtue happening*

*Be in Alignment*

*It is a happening!*

# Diamond Heart Energy Activations
## STEP 2: DNA Essential Program Downloads
# Communication

AFFIRMATIONS:

*I AM a Multi-Dimensional Being
of Communication
I AM a Being of Love Wisdom Power*

ESSENTIAL PROGRAM #2 DESCRIPTION:

Taking one's communications on to a higher level is largely a function of intention and the discipline of activating the receptors for this expanding awareness, and for responsible interactions and interplay. This opens centers in the brain and central nervous system that have corresponding centers in the higher dimensions or subtle bodies, and are balanced by the three-fold flame in the heart. The heart both centers the intuition and offers a foundation for new unfolding energy. The heart is the place where God communes with man.

The deeper the root the further the branches reach and spread out into the environment. This results in opening and unfolding one's ability to communicate with all of life: animals, plants, humans and angels. Get ready to be a part of the grand design that is divine and the free gift of the open heart. That is communication.

The higher self directly facilitates ALL of the shifts that we are asking for, and some of these processes can sometimes take days to weeks to integrate. The individuals working with Intention of spiritual up-liftment, begin working at deeper levels while sleeping; at this time individuals are sometimes taken to the retreats of the ascended masters, and receive energy or adjustments that are ever so precisely layered into the evolving consciousness, while preserving the integrity of life. Nothing happens in a vacuum. The mill of God grinds exceedingly slow yet it is precisely fine.

It has been suggested that we have seven Chakras and that these are located in the etheric body. Most are familiar with this area of spiritual science. As a biological species, we are shifting from a $3^{rd}$ dimensional life to a $5^{th}$ dimensional life-form that is more closely related to the causal body. One might find this shift to be as awkward as learning how to walk from the crawling stage. However it is natural once you have accomplished it. We are working on this now!

These downloads are a creative process and are part of a larger plan for the unfolding of man's great abilities. If you happen to be reading or listening to this material some good karma, or grace, has opened up for you and is opening up a next step.

The causal body is a little known body that holds all of your treasures, all of your credits from prior lives, and all the possibilities for wonder and achievement. It is only very recently that our whole biological life system that moves with the earth, has evolved into this energetic design; the corresponding centers within mankind are now capable of opening. This is from the seven chakra system in the etheric, to the 12 chakras of the causal body.

You can especially notice it amongst the young. They are reaching maturity much more quickly than older generations, and are into more things, including travel and personal development!

Communication is a heart and soul force phenomena. It is an unexpected call to a friend who needs you! It is an exercise done before the rain comes. It is the turning on the T.V. just in time to catch a special announcement. It is the purchase of a CD that inspires you deeply. It is a movie that critics trashed but you watched and found inspiring. Communication is the trying out of a new inspirational speaker that no one has heard about. It is a resonance thing. Communication is not about your ears. It is about your whole being—body, mind and spirit.

In the first Activation, your Trinity of Being was harmonized and brought into balance. Now you are going to receive an expanded version of your SELF, which is a step in the direction of your GIANT self, and you are going to learn to run with it. Why? Because you asked for it. How? This occurs through the over-lighting intelligence that we refer to as the Higher Self. Thank you for being here for the shift of the ages. Thank you for communicating your essence. Thank you for affirming the Trinity, for igniting the Three-Fold Flame of Wisdom-Love-Power and for communicating from this spiritual perspective.

## Affirmations

The affirmations are spoken in first person inclusive!

*I AM an open, intuitive, imaginative being.*

*I AM communicating from my truth, my being and essence.*

*I AM a heart centered being.*

*I AM expanding the three-fold flame of love, wisdom and power.*

*I AM a multi-dimensional being that communicates in light and sound.*

*I AM a point of light expanding into greater light in awareness.*

*I AM aware of my connections to all life.*

*I AM developing a receptivity and openness to all life.*

*I AM keeping an open mind, body, spirit for living fully.*

## Meditation

The *I AM* Meditation on Track 2 of the Activation #2 MP3 follows here.

## Meditations on the Virtues of the Diamond Heart

## #2

# Openness/Communication

Affirmations :

*I AM a Multi-Dimensional Being of Communication.*

*I AM a Being of Love-Wisdom-Power*

*I AM a center of expression for the primal will to good which eternally creates and sustains the universe*

    Let us open this consideration on Virtue with a recognition of the work of all the great thinkers and communicators of all time. To the great architects of the Vedas, the Bible including the book of Psalms, to the Tao Te Ch'ing, to the Buddha's Diamond Heart sutras, to the sermon on the mount and the master Jesus. To the inspired writings of Homer, of Socrates, Plato and Aristotle and to Lincoln. To the essays of R.W. Emerson, Whitman and Emily Dickinson. To Rumi, to Blake to Shakespeare to Kabir to Francis of Assisi to Chuang-Tzu, to Mozart and Bach. Ours is a rich inheritance because these beings were open to the soundless sound of silence and inspiration. Ours is a rich inheritance because they cared to share from heart to heart and mind to mind. Ours is a rich inheritance because in spite of all the odds, all the opposition and entropy, backlash and resistance, Openness and Communication remained the key note and guiding impulse for all of our forefathers and mothers. Ours is a rich inheritance if we care to open and to be Openness of Mind, Heart, Feeling and Expression.

## Listen Listen Listen
## Open Open Open

*All can be done when light's guiding touch champions the way,*
*And openness remains the disposition of the day.*
*Some say the best way to protect your heart is to open it.*
*All can be done.*
*You are destined to win, to conquer, to experience,*
*To be orphaned,*
*To sense, to be destroyed and to be rebuilt like the Phoenix rising;*
*Beauty and wonder never disturbing the fields.*
*The persistent thrill of a transfiguring touch flows out of time,*
*And touches your mind, as it always does when you open to it.*
*All can be done.*

*Listen Listen Listen*
*Open Open Open*

*All will be done now,*
*as there are cycles within cycles, wheels within wheels,*
*a gate ajar, opens to a new field of dreams.*
*Before sunrise, only an inert black quietude forms the back round*
*for your windowing.*
*Lean, look, labor, listen, learn and live*
*in the opalescence of all things.*
*One lucent corner magnifies the mystery*
*A glow along a moments magic mist,*
*Where junk yards claim your old experiences.*
*Next the new revelation outpours a sacred flame kiss.*
*Return to a slow miraculous fall into pillowy chance.*
*Listen Listen Listen*
*Open Open Open*

*All will be done as
invisible wandering hands replace the worn out stars and suns.*

*The glamour of an unreachable transcendency's crystal and light,
Cast beams and rays from wells of unfathomable depths
of infinity.
All is with All and in All and Communicates.
The smallest atom and the largest sun resonate,
And join in a dance of celebrated awake.
A grain of sand joins in the dance
And a large majestic bird flies overhead
as if by chance.
And gliding on wonder woven wings, looks and listens.
A perpetual sign and sound delivers,
The codes for this moment and begins,
Always thrilling for nerve and for skin.
Openness yields to the beginnings of all things
No excuses, must use it, open the wonder sails
Into the far-off waters of crystal and dream
Open keep opening you are not who you seem.
But born out of the great luminous immensity of Being.
Where rains wash and purify and Suns warm and dry,
And many and always the truth is spoken.
Eyes and ears, heart and mind
Fair finer when they arrive open*

*Listen, Listen, Listen
Open, Open, Open
And Communication Happens.*

# Openness/Communication is our Second Diamond Heart Virtue

As the story goes there were two men traveling together: an old and wise Zen monk and a bean farmer. They traveled well together although they rarely spoke. The quietness and silence of the all pervading sky was good enough company for the monk. And watching his every step, face towards the ground, was the habit of the farmer. A chance meeting with another enlightened monk who had been living far off in the mountains for years and years was almost too joyous for the old Zen monk to handle. Each folding their hands together upon their chests, celebrating, bowing reverently, tears flowing, heart's radiating. Finally the enlightened monk raised his hand and pointed to the sky in the ancient monks custom of acknowledging, All is One, Wholeness is the order of life, the Eternal Truths can never be spoken, Love is the creative force behind all creation, from the Primordial Silence comes the root sounds of/for creation, and all things flow out of the One and return to the One.

The bean farmer quickly pulled a coil of rope from his knapsack—just in case the enlightened monk was crazy or something. He began pacing feverishly. Finally both monks fell over laughing hysterically, realizing if you empty yourself and open yourself to the sky of possibility, you can find enlightenment that is beyond description. And, by contrast, there is very little you will capture with a small coil of rope!

Openness is not something you do. It is an open sky that you come to realize, just is.

It is not a strategy for getting ahead or an effort applied when you fall behind. Doing nothing is easy, like walking under open the sky. Being open is just like water not rushing anywhere, it becomes clear. Communication is just the breathing in and out. When two minds meet hardly a word need to be spoken and yet communication happens. Two people meet in the heart and there is the recognition of the heart of it ALL as nature, as sky, as people.

Virtue is not something applied to another for this reason or that, or for some payoff or benefit down the road. Openness is the road. Openness is the sky. Openness is the way because it is in the nature of all things enlightened, or natural, or normal to be, open.

## Be Open

*Be Open and All will remain with the Tao.*
*Communicate openness by being in harmony as the Self,*
*As a simple and natural condition.*
*Be Open and stars and suns will come and go*
*But you will remain as Openness/Communication*

*Be Open as it is in the Tao of All things.*
*Communicate Openness even sometimes as or in Silence*
*And the seasons will arrive on time and as expected*
*Be Open and notice the connectedness of all things*
*Your footsteps will sound a symphony*
*of wonder and delight for those who love*
*the simplicity of things as*
*Openness and Communication*
*happens.*

Diamond Heart Energy Activations
STEP 3: DNA Essential Program Downloads

# Super-Consciousness Mind and the Higher Self Guidance & Intuition

**AFFIRMATION:**

*I AM Being Divinely Guided*

**ESSENTIAL PROGRAM #3 DESCRIPTION:**

For every individual in God's great kingdom there is a Guardian Angel. But, even before we get to this, we have at our disposal rich, deep and incredible internal resources that are based on lifetimes of growth and development. There are children who have walked up to a piano and started playing and, although genius is a hard thing to manage, it happens amongst us. There are people who can visit a strange city—having never before stepped foot into such a place—who can go exactly to where they need to go without instruction.

There are countless examples of the super conscious mind and every one has some experience of a direct insight as a result of a sudden flash. These are the direct result of either the Guidance, the Brilliance, or from accessing information from the outside environment or any combination of the three! The aspect of you that lives beyond conditioned reality is remarkable and accessible. It has no doubt, no fear, and no distressful or painful cravings. It knows everything that you need to be doing, perusing, unfolding and directing at all times.

This Activation takes the intention of the first session of *Aligning the Trinity* and the second activation of *Communications* and moves us from an open heart and a biological being and expands us to a Spiritual Being who accepts the gifts of the creator and can be divinely guided. Being divinely guided, one can think more clearly and solve problems quickly. One can seek out the causes of pain and suffering in one's own life and uproot them. One can and will improve one's relationships with all beings. One can become more and more excited in the use of new and refreshing strategies for bringing balance to one's personal affairs. One can develop a greater sense of purpose and unfold his or her unique destiny.

By the time a person has reached the age of 18, the core beliefs of one's family and culture have been cast upon them so many times that there is no way out but UP. All good things flow from above downward and from inside out. We ask, seek and knock and gain access to a higher, better, clearer directing intelligence.

In the first Activation your Trinity of Being was harmonized and brought into balance. In the second activation we received and explored an expanded version of your SELF. Now we are stepping into the expanded awareness of the higher self and the super-conscious mind, accessing the order of life and the guidance, flowing always in our direction.

**AFFIRMATIONS:**

*I AM a being Divinely Guided and I move in balance, in harmony, with each step I take.*

*I accept my Divine inheritance and rely upon this at all times.*

*I will invoke a higher order of being, of guidance, into my thinking and feeling.*

*I AM a being of multidimensional capability that is attracting the appropriate people, places and circumstances into all my affairs.*

*I AM a being Divinely Guided!*

*I accept the exalted state of the super-conscious mind.*

*I transcend my own and others' limited thinking, by invoking the resources of my divine guidance.*

*I AM a being of infinite potential and I affirm that each day of my life is dedicated to unfolding the highest aspects of my true, real and eternal nature!*

*By grace so shall guidance prevail. I focus my intention and surrender the outcome to God.*

**I AM a being Divinely guided!**

**MEDITATION**

The *I AM* Meditation on Track 2 of Activation #3 MP3 follows here.

# Meditations on the Virtues of the Diamond Heart

# #3

# Intuition

# Super-Consciousness Mind and the Higher Self Guidance & Intuition

**Affirmations:** *I AM Being Divinely Guided*
*Through me it's unfailing wisdom takes form in word and deed*

As I look at my lists of virtues from a variety of sources, it is interesting to note that our next virtue is not on any of them directly. In other words, the word INTUITION does not show up. However there are a few other words that might lean in the direction of this quality.

*Wisdom* is one word but wisdom is usually the result of much experience. *Synthesis* is another word that might approach our inquiry, but this also may focus our attention on outside things. So clearly, we can assume that we are contributing to the exploration of Virtue, through recognition, assimilation, expression and intuition. And, is there a state that one must enter before one's intuition is truly focused, like a peaceful one perhaps?

The following is from the Tattiriya Upanishads, a group of writings at the end of the Vedas. The authors are unknown and even the date of emergence is back at least five thousand years ago and possibly much older.

*May the Lord of the Day grant us peace.*
*May the Lord of the Night grant us peace.*
*May the Lord of Sight grant us peace.*
*May the Lord of Might grant us peace.*
*May the Lord of Speech grant us peace.*
*May the Lord of Space grant us peace.*
*I bow down to Brahman, source of power.*
*I will speak the truth and follow the law.*
*Guard me and my teacher against all harm.*
*Guard me and my teacher against all harm.*

One's intuition knows to ask the right questions, to go to the right sources, to ask for or seek the optimal circumstances; honoring the request for *US* acknowledges the unity of life.

A thief can have intuition but not peace. There are also two schools of thought on psychic development. One is to "seek ye first the kingdom of God and all good things will be added to you", or develop spiritually and the psychic gifts will open properly. The other methods do not interest us here.

Asking for peace may somehow imply that we can only have peace as a result of harmony, of balance, of prosperity, of order, of health. We might even look at Intuition as a culmination of alignment, going to Source, and of Openness/Communication as having taken the responsibility for one's ideas, motivations and actions. One places the request/ consideration/ concern upon the altar of Truth, before the eyes of the creator, includes humanity with sincerity and, of course, in the rich tradition of India, honors the teacher, the liberator, the Guru, and Brahman or Source.

It is interesting to note that from our third activation we see this Activation takes the intention of the first session of *Aligning the Trinity*, and the second activation of *Communications*, and then moves us from an open heart and a biological being and expands us to a Spiritual Being, who accepts the gifts of the creator and can be divinely guided". Good *Intuition* is the result of having done the real work, explored all the angles, synthesized the relative considerations and invoked the highest order of being.

# Fate

*Your fate may wish to follow a foreseen and predictable road,*
*But your destiny/mastery could free you another.*
*A blind will fall and fall upon the goal,*
*For greater spirits a blazed access avoids the trouble.*
*If a face is formed in stone and doom,*
*Nary a flower— sweet shall one summer watch bloom.*
*One cannot hear the footsteps of the softly descending rain,*
*If the sounds of past and future boom,*
*Loosing the Eternal Nowness of things.*
*Often left to trial again and again and again,*
*And sitting behind clumsy and loud, hastening hooves.*
*Looking up, one may see the ease of brighter days.*
*Beacon lights wallowing on green velvet hills.*
*Far off voices have psalms to sing of heavenly praise,*
*Seeds to sow, birds to sing and gentle wind to carry them.*
*If only to align with a magnificent will,*
*A will of wonder, of knowledge and might.*
*Fires eternal lit, burning in a wide, open blaze,*
*Shine a light on the lightness of things.*
*Lightness of being, lightness of seeing,*
*Lightness of feeling, of shape and of color and tone.*
*Who knew of this hidden spirit's choice?*
*Who knew of the deep recessed voice?*
*Who first called for the flag to be raised?*
*When was this treasure first elevated and praised?*
*Who sent the morning light our way?*
*To loll and to ease our sense and place.*

*Anyway, who?*
*Let your own secret soul reveal this,*
*Let your own inner mind ascend to this,*
*Let it be your own being's decree a knowing and a bliss,*
*To own and to live, to love and to learn*
*Intuitively.*
*From inside inspiration*
*To live, to love and to learn*
*Intuitively.*

# Diamond Heart Energy Activations
## STEP 4: DNA Essential Program Downloads
# Co-Creation, Talents & Productivity

**AFFIRMATION:**

*I am a magical being
of Infinite Creativity*

**ESSENTIAL PROGRAM #4 DESCRIPTION:**

This activation focuses on the gifts of the soul and of the spirit. These gifts may align with many of the gifts that are on display in our world of art, music, theatre, science, healing, divination, prophesy, dream interpretation, public speaking, leadership, motivational training and teaching in any capacity.

These may also include areas of development that are lacking in your life where you are being given special dispensations, because good karma for circumstances are arising to support you, to get along with it, with physical support and inner support. Many a creation comes from the *NO Where* to the *NOW Here*. Ideas and creative urges flow at most unexpected times and from unexpected places.

When you open up to the rainbow fields of all possibility, you invoke the support of the elementals and the angels and guides. At any moment the over-lighting energies may move you, push you, pull you, urge you to allow inspiration to flow like NEVER before. Be prepared to see your finest work come out. Are you ready to accept this support? *Yes.* Are you willing to move forward? *Yes.* Are you able to make this decision? *Yes.*

In the first activation your trinity of being was harmonized and brought into balance. In the second activation you received and explored an expanded version of your SELF. In the third we began stepping into the expanded awareness of the higher self and the superconscious mind and accessing the order of life and the guidance flowing always in your direction. Now in this, our fourth step, we are going to bring this intelligence forward into form through co-creation, expression of our talents and productivity affirming *I AM a magical being of Infinite Creativity*.

**AFFIRMATIONS:**

*I AM a being endowed with the gifts of the Creator!*

*I AM a being of Infinite Intelligence!*

*All that is in the field of cosmic possibility, is there for you to shape and mold to your unique design.*

*I AM and have come a long way to balance my Trinity, to open my heart nd expand the three fold flame.*

*I AM a being of multi-dimensional communication ability who brings creative genius into focus when desired.*

*I AM fashioned like a diamond reflecting color and imagination into all your creations.*

*I AM making decisions that will continue to open up greater avenues for self-expression.*

*I AM able to access the gifts of the past and focus them here and now.*

*I AM learning now at an accelerated rate with minimal instruction.*

*I AM learning quite naturally to simply absorb knowledge, inspiration, images, and essences and form them in my creations.*

*I AM a co-creator, partnered with the higher dimensions of light and sound, and bring about sacred offerings for the joy and honor of life.*

**I AM a Magical being of Infinite Creativity.**

MEDITATION

The *I AM* Meditation on Track 2 of Activation #4 MP3 follows here.

# Meditations on the Virtues of the Diamond Heart

# #4

# Co-Creation, Talents & Productivity

Affirmation: *I am a magical being of Infinite Creativity*
Filled with the understanding of it's perfect law,
*I AM* guided, moment by moment along the path of liberation.

Benjamin Franklin had the word of *industry* on his list of virtues and this probably most closely indentifies with our triple virtue of *Co-Creation, Talents and Productivity*. We are reminded of the story of the scientists and God participating in their creation challenge.

God does and we redo. But now here we have the dynamic of co-creation and a more multidimensional consideration. The writer here had not played the guitar for 14 years when he was directed to meditate and ask God for direction in life. It was suggested that he do this in the early morning for three weeks and the result would be an answer of a specific direction. After three weeks he was playing and singing and chanting. After three years he had produced seven music CD's and a 12 CD set of the Diamond Heart Energy Activations which utilizes sound vibrational healing/transmissions in conjunction with "*I AM* Source Energy" to perform the magic of up-grading DNA. Performing ceremony is our part, assistance by the guides is heaven's part, and this synthesis is a form of co-creation. Now Intuition and Industry give birth as if at each step is a new flowering, like a Fibonacci number series of one plus one is two, one plus two is three, two plus three is five. By including the step we are in with the previous step we advance to the next step as a flowering of fragrance, of substance, of form and possibility. The Golden Mean of *proporti*.

So co-creation is a multidimensional, inspirational and dynamic affair that can open one to the magical hidden SELF within each of us to bring forth OUR unique gifts, destinies, abilities and contributions. Return to our original plan of working in concert with nature, with heaven, for purposes which lend a beauty, a harmony and a balance to the world, co-contribute through *Co-Creativity, Talents and Productivity*.

## A Magical Being of Creativity Awakes

*Before the gods wake up*
*Nothing happens in the morning.*
*No sun to light up our way.*
*No angels' wings and no birds to sing,*
*No gentle winds resounding the day.*
*Then a power of boundless Self awake,*
*Then a conscious All that there is,*
*From silence moves to magnificence.*
*From womb to birth to mystery to chance,*
*A great and awesome power beacons to you.*
*A kaleidoscope of un-bodied bright,*
*A volcano of heat and of fire,*
*Liquid and dancing filled with Light.*

*A magical being of creativity awakes.*

*You rub your eyes to cast the demons of sleep out.*
*And try to stretch and begin and recall,*
*Just which dreams will be erected today,*
*Just how many might fall.*
*A smile seems to wash over you,*
*You stir the bowl of crystal like possibilities.*
*And drink a sweetened cup of remembering bliss,*
*Orphaned and driven out of the comfort of dreams,*

*Today I must again find my place.*
*A hope is stolen away in a place that barely dared to be,*
*As if a soul once asleep longed to move.*
*And a sense is born within the darkness depths*
*That overcomes the crowded tablets of the past.*

*A magical being of creativity awakes.*

*A Now Moment of velvety touch,*
*A Now Moment of Now What too,*
*Presence with anxious.*
*Advance on the slumbering crystal roads,*
*A long long lone road for hesitating shoes and feet,*
*I AM I Think or at least I long to be.*
*I feel I guess a freedom to want to look and to see.*
*I grasp some seed in here with my naked fingered hands,*
*And scatter them out upon a field of fragrant billowy green.*
*A gentle rain of wondrous wide stepped intentions,*
*A gentle push of hidden but redeeming focused things,*
*And sounds of creation each lung sings,*
*And sings out a harmony.*
*Body turns back to face a daunting dawning infinity ray,*
*I AM I Feel or at least I long to be*
*A magical being of infinite light,*
*Of infinite creativity.*

*I AM A Being of Magical Infinity Creativity.*

*Co-Creation, Talents & Productivity never works alone,*
*but Invokes a higher power and unfolds from the Synthesis of Alignment,*
*Openness/Communication, Intuition into Creativity.*

*I AM A Being of Magical Infinity Creativity*

*I AM*

*Co-Creation plus Talents Plus Productivity flowers*
*Magical Creativity*

## Diamond Heart Energy Activations
## STEP 5: DNA Essential Program Downloads
# My Covenants with Life, Purpose and Plan

**AFFIRMATION:**

*I AM a focus of light and energy keeping all my covenants with life.*

**ESSENTIAL PROGRAM #5 DESCRIPTION:**

From the great sage Lao Tzu, who predated Jesus and Buddha, we have an appropriate saying:

*The Highest good is like water. Water gives life to the ten thousand things and does not strive. It flows in places men reject and thus it is like the Tao.*

*In dwelling, be close to the land.*

*In meditation, go deep in the heart.*

*In dealing with others, be gentle and kind!*

*In speech be true.*

*In ruling be just.*

*In business be competent.*

*In action, watch the timing.*

This download is focusing the synthesis of the first four downloads and bringing it in on a more personal level. The Divine Plan is the same for all sentient beings—to keep on unfolding towards perfection. However, our own contracts for this life are personal. You choose your parents, your time of birth, and place of birth, for the expressed purpose of getting it on in *THIS LIFE*, not later.

To recap our activation thus far we have:

- First, we *Aligned the Trinity*.
- Second, *Activated the Heart* and the three-fold flame of Love, Wisdom and Power.
- Third, we expanded our *Communication* network by expanding consciousness and made a determination that we are guided by the inner plane master teachers and angels.
- Fourth, we activated the program and DNA sequence for co-creation and creativity.

Now we are ready to take a spin around the block so to speak. We are ready to receive, to look at relationships, careers, interests and invocations with a more discriminating eye. We want to take on the tasks before us with passion and conviction. We are asking for the energy to wake up, to move forward, to learn the lessons of this school of life and participate as fully as possible. In honoring this sacred moment of choice we will reflect with you on the following affirmations:

**AFFIRMATIONS:**

*I AM a spiritual being having a physical experience.*

*I AM made of star stuff, and shine as bright as light.*

*I AM a unique, individualized aspect of the One Being, God.*

*I have place on God's great earth and in heaven, designed especially for me.*

*I AM in relationship with life and all its aspects are sacred.*

*No one does it quite like you, you are the original you.*

*I AM a preserver who nourishes, a regenerator who grows and evolves.*

*I AM rejoicing in achievements, however small or large they may be.*

*I AM set in INTENTION, to bring about a profound sense of balance and harmony.*

*I AM a Being of Alignment, of Communication, of Intuition and Creativity moving with the Tao of things, with the proper flow of meaning, purpose and imagination.*

*Whatever hurdles are placed upon my path, I leap over and establish balance and equanimity. All is with God and all is good!*

*I AM the NOW momentum of this life, and every door I need to walk through will open for me when I ask, seek and knock!*

*Now is my now moment of Awakening and Awareness!*

**Affirmation: *I AM a focus of light and energy keeping all my covenants with life.***

**MEDITATION**

(Use a Tibetan bowl)

Track 2 of the #5 Activation MP3 follows here.

## Meditations on the Virtues of the Diamond Heart

## #5

# My Covenants with Life, Purpose and Plan

Affirmation: *I AM* a focus of light and energy
keeping all my covenants with life.
From the exhaustless riches of it's limitless substance
I draw all things needful
both spiritual and material.

It is not as if someone handed you the broom and asked you to sweep the floor. You are already standing on it. But your giant self is calling and saying remember me, find me!

Wake up and remember what it is that you have come here to do. Wow! What a consideration, altogether possible, but not at all probable unless some new action is taken, unless a new agreement is reached, unless the sound of the Still Small Voice is suddenly appreciated, unless a new and exciting focus becomes the habit, the natural, the heart.

Science says you are using just a small part of the potential energy, like less than ten percent. Deepak Chopra says only five percent of the people who do his trainings follow through. But Jesus said "Be perfect, even as your Father in heaven is perfect".

Don't blame him this time or expect him to die again for your sins. It isn't going to happen.

This is you at bat. This is your time with the reins. This has to mean that it is all together possible to get it right, do it right, make it right, fit it right. That is the opportunity. This is the life. Now is the time. Where do I sign up? This is exciting. Remember, courage is action in the face of fear. It takes wisdom, love and power to succeed, to synergize.

This 5th Virtue could not have been generated without the virtue of Alignment, Openness/Communication, Intuition, Co-Creation-Talent-Productivity as our predecessors, no way.

We are not exploring cleanliness with the broom. We have a larger agenda, a deeply personal agenda, this is my own soul mission that I alone have conceived and master planned. I alone must discover and implement. This a man up mission. Destiny is an exalted road way beyond the well traveled ones bearing the boredom of chance and circumstances. This is a spiral staircase to the sun of excellence and freedom. It has the sound of your own voice only, and only you have the key to unlock the treasure chest of distinction, liberation, freedom and expression.

*Enough to Be Still, To Know, and To be Silent*
*Enough to Be Still, To Know, and To be Silent*
*Enough to Be Still, To Know, and To be Silent*

## In a Deep Oneness

*In a deep Oneness of all things that are,*
*It should be easy to follow one's dreams.*
*Not building sand castles that don't last very long,*
*Oceans wash and pound upon rock and upon the sands.*
*Alone we move in our destinies of chance.*
*As if someone outside us could point us the way.*
*Around some assemble a wall to protect them,*
*Which collapses brick by brick by brick one stormy day.*
*All can be seen to the eye that is single.*
*All could be revealed in the sound of the song of the sea.*
*But into the shallow streams one's cells go to mingle,*
*Flinging oneself into the hazards of sleep, loss and or delay.*
*A self-creation without direction or cause or pause*
*World-shaped without memory or skill,*
*Do not render or surrender to this tiny self will.*

*In a deep Oneness,*

*All may be seen if you close your eyes, turn inward.*
*All could be known if the little mind be still.*
*All could be done for glory for family for country.*
*A flag is hoisted upon a flowering and green sloping hill.*
*Revelation, jubilation, participation a plausible plan.*
*Formulas for freedom, passion for power, only love,*
*Love action may pilot your gliding probability craft.*

*Upward Into a sky of sun-shaped possibilities,*
*Above the clouds of limitation, dreariness, sleep.*
*Action must be taken, words must be spoken,*
*A focus, an intention, a promise to keep,*
*A thousand times, a thousand fold*
*Comes the promise of the light.*

*In a deep Oneness,*

*Give up that which wants to prevent you,*
*Mind you, destroy or delay you.*
*Release the hold of that which is not at all very bright.*
*Nothing escapes the law of cause and effect,*
*Except by grace.*
*By a cycle soon to be finished,*
*Be guided by a vast and loving intuitive sight.*
*Cast out all invading energy.*
*Close the doors to all of questionable intent.*
*Shift a few habits and behaviors,*
*And structure a vision of cosmic delight.*

*An exhaustless river pours forth before you,*
*Drink one cup at a time of this wine and be fine.*
*Commission a new mighty heart message,*
*Of purpose, of pleasure, of power, of peace.*
*Of one that may focus your welcoming spirit,*
*Then into this diamond heart one's own self*
*must be released.*
*Into a deep Oneness as things, as being, as destiny,*
*As opportunity emerge into light.*
*Into a deep Oneness.*

Diamond Heart Energy Activations
STEP 6: DNA Essential Program Downloads

# Organization and Cooperation

**AFFIRMATION:**

*I AM RE-defining RE-developing and Re-directing my personal database to be in Alignment with my higher self.*

**ESSENTIAL PROGRAM #6 DESCRIPTION:**

The super-conscious mind knows a lot about the road ahead. The sub-conscious mind remembers every thing that has ever happened. The conscious mind only needs a little of that information at a time. So here we see the need for a program and function that will keep all things relevant, expedient, cohesive and accessible. Too much information is not a good thing. Also everyone experiences both unhappy and painful events that they no longer need to energize!

Your Higher Self can assist you in the remembering things without the harmful emotions attached. If you fly above the clouds so to speak, you do not have to worry about the rain. As you continue to work in earnest for the purpose of greater "*I AM*" self-discovery and utilize the Violet Flame of Transformation, your four lower bodies will contain less and less of the discord both personal and planetary!

Also there are huge energy packets that continue to float into our atmosphere that are assisting us to flow with the planetary ascension process. This program will keep you current and keep you clear within the parameters of your personal identity, agenda and inspirations. Activation of this program will also assist you to focus more of only what you need from outside sources keeping your energy and attention stream-lined and potently focused, as well as balanced mentally and emotionally.

To recap our activation thus far we have: First, we *Aligned the Trinity*. Second, *Activated the Heart* and the three-fold flame of Love, Wisdom and Power. Third, we expanded our *Communication* network by expanding consciousness and making a determination that we are (can be) guided by the inner plane master teachers and angels. Fourth, we activated the program and DNA sequence for *Co-Creation and Creativity*. The Fifth program and activation focused our *Personal Covenants and the Divine Plan*. Here in the sixth phase we are *Becoming more Synergistic with Levels of Consciousness*. We are redefining, redeveloping and redirecting intelligence, devotion, attention and emotion. This is a great I.D.E.A. to have Intelligence, Dedication, Emotion and Attention all moving in the same direction.

## Affirmations

*I AM RE defining, RE developing and RE directing my personal database to be in alignment with my higher self.*

(Read the above statement to alternate with each statement below.)

*I AM the balance of power, precision and promise.*

*I AM a well organized being focused in the present and drawing from all possible resources.*

*I AM the release of the past and any and all harmful programs.*

*I AM the Spirit of Loving Forgiveness and the Violet Flame in action around and within to blaze and spin and expand consciousness.*

*I AM my boundary clear and well defined.*

*I AM the access to all necessary information naturally, intuitively in response to the need for development and balanced expression.*

*I AM walking my path in the direction of my choice for the highest possible reward.*

*I AM maintaining effortlessly and freely all my past experience to empower my play.*

*I AM I AM I AM that I AM.*

**I AM RE-defining RE-developing and RE-directing my personal database to be in Alignment with my higher self.**

## Meditation

The *I AM* Meditation on Track 2 of the Activation #6 MP3 follows here.

## Meditations on the Virtues of the Diamond Heart

## #6

# Organization, Cooperation and Momentum

*Affirmations: I AM RE-defining RE-developing and RE-directing my personal database to be in alignment with my higher self.*

*I recognize the manifestation of the undeviating justice in all the circumstances of my life.*

*I recognize the externalization of my inner state of mind.*

Momentum is KEY for this meditation. Again we recognize that our virtue is not the horizontal 3-D action—however balanced and harmonized—of extension to another, such as the virtues of patience, compassion or charity. Our virtue is always the flowing movement or realization of the trinity and synthesis of quality. It is a virtue of Self Awareness plus Existence. It is the Ready, Aim and then Fire. It is an awakening and invocation of a vertical impulse that flows forth to our co-creations, from the *No Where* to the *Now Here*. Your creations are born from thin air. First, there was a movement in the heart, then the mind, and now your feet and hands are busy.

You may hear the faint but fantastic celestial sounds. You feel the wind upon your brow. You sense a wave of magnetic energy rising and riding up through your body. An electronic pulse from the sun of possibilities and something begins to reassemble. Suddenly, an alignment is upon you, and a whisper of a promising touch and color and shape and sound. The architect child has grown to a fuller measure. Suddenly your brush begins to paint you. Your song now is sung. You are a radio broadcasting a symphony of delight and thrill. Just where does it come from and how did it get here? You have tapped into the jet stream of all the possibilities of dream and design. You strap your self in and look out for any signs of a familiar surrounding and go with it! Something wants to move and keep moving, to breathe and to stretch and create.

You light a fire under the sticks, the lumber and stories of the past, and fire up a sparkle of spontaneity and essence, magic, mindfulness, momentum. Each day a new canvas, and every hour a color or shape, and each moment a breath of creation; your channel has become alive again, inside your tube of White Light, a new movement defines you. Go and follow your heart. The key word is *Go!*

# Light and Life

*If the life you lead conceals the light that you are, you lose.*
*When you walk, walk tall and let your soul guide your shoes.*
*The soul of a man is greater than any fate.*
*Remember, Gandhi was thrown from a train.*
*Still he was not troubled being late,*
*He arrived right on time at his destination of freedom.*
*He carried humanity upon his back*

*The day lightbringer walks through the night*
*to his morning of victory and glow.*
*Bless the mountain that you are standing upon,*
*And the wind and the rain and the snow.*
*Walk softly and carry a big stick.*
*Wearing a crown*
*Of suns and stars,*
*Of galaxies and moons,*
*Gaze inside your robe of experience,*
*A little star dust you must sprinkle*
*On these hollowed grounds.*

*Jump in and swim at the river of chance,*
*Avoid the alligators of despair.*
*Inside of you is a fountain of youth,*
*Even as around you all seems to be transitioning.*
*Another cycle another swim,*
*Some one has turned on the moving lights again.*
*Some say this is the greatest time to be alive,*

*Now, is there really any other?*
*Now, is there really any other?*

*Cycles within cycles, wheels within wheels*
*Your SELF the point of stillness*
*It is all moving to thrill.*
*From the cradle of your innocence and power*
*Comes forth a sun,*
*A life giving life loving One.*
*And wisdom can only flow from experience.*
*And love can only flow from your heart.*
*And power can only flow from the one source you know,*
*The nameless One,*
*The One some simply call great.*

*Deep within you now, remember your ancestors.*
*Deep within you, remember your source.*
*Deep within you throw the switch,*
*That lights the light that lights,*
*The lights that lights your torch.*
*A glowing being is a liberated one,*
*Who calls forth electrons and protons*
*Just for fun.*
*To assemble his dream-fired*
*Fantasies and co-creations,*
*All to the glory of the One,*
*Go,*
Now!

## Meditations on the Diamond Heart

*When you discover a key to one's liberation and freedom*
*Can you not put it on the table?*
*Acknowledging those who accept it gladly*
*Can you not share their enthusiasm?*
*Discussing with those the advantages and considerations,*
*Can you not have patience, focus and generosity?*
*Observing those closed and fickle of fate or fortune*
*Can you remain free of any judgment and condemnation?*
*Allowing the seasons to guide us,*
*Following a lightness of touch,*
*Releasing any hold that might bind us,*
*Increasing with humble surrendering.*
*Focusing freedom for peace,*
*Into a new and higher ethic.*
*Where a divine wind fills sails,*
*Into a new and higher ethic,*
*Where a divine will prevails.*

## Diamond Heart Energy Activations
### STEP 7: DNA Essential Program Downloads
# Synergy and Fluidity

AFFIRMATION:

*I AM a Multidimensional Being
Shape Shifting with Synergistic Fluidity*

ESSENTIAL PROGRAM #7 DESCRIPTION:

**The Reading**

"When you are upgrading and making adjustments, integrating and adapting to new sensations, information, light and life then all is as it should be."

*Then one is truly in the present, in the beauty, in the flow.*

*Then one is truly in the present, in the beauty, in the flow.*

*Then one is truly in the present, in the beauty, in the flow.*

We have asked the universe and God and the great collective *I AM* Presence to enter in on behalf of our forward motion, on behalf of our unfolding the great and wonder powers of co-creation. This, the seventh session, places us at the point of NOW return. Enough energy and light has been downloaded into your system that you are beginning to climb to greater heights. Therefore, the program that makes corrections for your acceleration needs to be activated, so that automatically, your systems will turn towards the true north; so that your signal-to-noise ratio is always at smooth running and minimal degree of disturbance.

Synergy and fluidity, synergy and fluidity like water and the river flowing, *I AM* the waters of life. Like the Earth, *I AM* a mountain of faith. Like the Sacred Fire, I sparkle and crackle and turn and spin. Like the Air, *I AM* a tornado of enthusiasm and possibility. Like the Etheric, I reflect a greater light, like the Sun. *I AM* alive with feeling and energy, and aligned with the One Spirit. One to will and One to wonder, synergistically with fluidity.

To recap our activations thus far we have: First, *Aligned the Trinity*. Second, *Activated the Heart* and the three-fold flame of Love, Wisdom and Power. Third, we expanded our *Communication* network by expanding consciousness and making a determination that we are (can be) guided by the inner plane master, teachers and angels. Fourth, we activated the program and DNA sequence for *Co-Creation and Creativity*. The Fifth program and activation focused our personal covenants and the Divine Plan, and in the Sixth phase we became more *Integrated with Levels of Consciousness*. Now at the Seventh phase we enter into smooth running, effortless adjusting and more masterful action and responses.

There are bigger mountains to climb, bigger fish to fry. The flow of energy information through our energy circuits is becoming more and more refined, accepting finer waves of light and the powers for transformation that lie therein. Synergy and fluidity are the sound/word symbols for the activation today. This Essential program is being activated.

### Affirmations

*I AM a Being upgrading and continuously moving to the higher ground.*

**I AM a Multidimensional Being, Shape Shifting with Synergistic Fluidity.**

*I AM a way shower peacefully moving along my destiny path.*

**I AM a Multidimensional Being, Shape Shifting with Synergistic Fluidity.**

*I AM an open channel of light, magnetics, radiation and wonder.*

**I AM a Multidimensional Being, Shape Shifting with Synergistic Fluidity.**

*The universe pours through my mind and body and spirit and creations.*

**I AM a Multidimensional Being, Shape Shifting with Synergistic Fluidity.**

*I AM a Star walker bringing color and magic to this life.*

**I AM a Multidimensional Being, Shape Shifting with Synergistic Fluidity.**

*I AM open, receptive, willing and able to focus fantastic new ideas.*

**I AM a Multidimensional Being, Shape Shifting with Synergistic Fluidity.**

*I AM a grateful co-creator charged with positive atoms and electrons of spiraling passion.*

**I AM a Multidimensional Being, Shape Shifting with Synergistic Fluidity.**

*I AM adjusting, up grading, Making Corrections and Automatic Overrides with grace and fluidity.*

**I AM a Multidimensional Being, Shape Shifting with Synergistic Fluidity.**

*I AM a conscious Being of each now moment being where I should be when I should be.*

**I AM a Multidimensional Being, Shape Shifting with Synergistic Fluidity.**

*I AM guided to a right and unfolding personal destiny in he light.*

**I AM a Multidimensional Being, Shape Shifting with Synergistic Fluidity.**

*I AM a shape shifter of pulsating light, executing precision and equilibrium.*

**I AM a Multidimensional Being, Shape Shifting with Synergistic Fluidity.**

*When you are upgrading and making adjustments, integrating and adapting to new sensations, information, light and life, then all is as it should be. Then, one is truly in the present, in the beauty, in the flow.*

**I AM a Multidimensional Being, Shape Shifting with Synergistic Fluidity.**

### Meditation

The *I AM* Meditation on Track 2 of Activation #7 MP3 follows here.

# Meditations on the Virtues of the Diamond Heart
# #7
# Synergy and Fluidity and Beauty

Affirmation:

*I AM a Multidimensional Being, Shape Shifting with Synergistic Fluidity*
*In All things great and small, I see the beauty of the divine expression.*

Especially here and now it is important to borrow this statement from the program descriptions, and I quote, "When *I AM* upgrading and making adjustments, integrating and adapting to new sensation, information, light and life, then all is as it should be. Then one is present in the beauty and the flow". If you were in a coma these activations would not really make a difference for you. Short of that, the benefit of invoking the higher energies in times such as we are in on the planet is most beneficial, as we move into new and more and more subtle dimensions of ALL Creative Light. To say mandatory might be a bit presumptuous. To say evolutionary, transformative and timely is probably very appropriate. The sun is always traveling from East to West. NO stops; NO stutter steps; just fluidity with energy and light. How would you like to be that consistent?

# Of Beauty, Synergy and Fluidity

*Of Beauty, Synergy and Fluidity*
*The journeying wheels that spin at dawn before the world*
*Wakes up are built of shine and chrome.*
*Secret souls plot and plan an excellence not widely known,*
*Or appreciated close to home.*
*Or even in the times of their own, lives.*
*Sailing ships carried Gabran and the prophets words across the sea.*
*But he was deep at rest when they were carried here to thee.*
*Mevlana Jalladin Rumi was a poet of considerable import,*
*everybody knows,*

*600 years ago most folks could not even read.*
*Does matter mold our earthly life?*
*Or does a dream or two break through our mystic minds,*
*And lead the blind man to see?*
*Nature's drives transcended momentarily,*
*Find compelling fates of their own.*
*Beauty, Synergy and Fluidity!*
*Far heard off chariots leave a spray of magic in the dust.*
*Far heard off volcanoes of crackle and fire.*
*Hills wallowing off in a bright open haze,*
*Have long known seeds of desire.*
*Summer's heaven's sea mists have longed to be kissed,*
*By voices that like to carry to thee.*
*Passages, poems, psalms and shadows of seed light,*
*To build in the soil and rock,*
*Of a timeless opal reality.*

*Life is not bread and*
*Love's poem's pages have no ages,*
*But leave an undeniable rose glistened*
*mark upon the heart.*
*You leave your tower of complacency and journey,*
*through a forgotten memory, alone,*
*a thoughtful brooding solemn trance*
*opens to a wide slow gliding moon, arise.*
*You are the first to arrive.*
*Another moment of Beauty, Synergy and Fluidity,*

*This moon I'll ask to report back to me,*
*of All the secrets of each fountain's splash,*
*of each river's bend, of each mountain's climb,*

*Of each silk feathered golden eagle's head,*

*An owl makes her presence known to me.*

*Of close clinging clasps of kings and of queens,*

*Of white cobblestoned roads that lead to the sea,*

*Of a glad smile in the forest's tremendous heart,*

*Of the ageless wisdom of the Pyramids and Sphinx.*

*Of all joy on Earth and Heaven's beatitude,*

*I'll share I swear I promised the moon.*

*If only for a sense*

*Of Beauty, Synergy and Fluidity*

*To Arise, Within Me.*


**The seventh meditation on the virtues** is the dynamic action of Synergy and Fluidity as Beauty.

There is a Sufi saying that *"Reason is powerless in the expression of love. Love alone is capable of revealing the presence and truth of love, and of being a lover. It is like the moment between the bud and the rose, it is only known to the roses"*. Such is the way of this ascension process, a movement from self to SELF, from functioning within a seven chakra energetic system to an opening of 12 chakras or energy centers in the light body. We are moving from a carbon based life system to a crystalline based life system. There are 12 strands of DNA and there are 12 etheric templates that we access as we invoke the downloads. We do them over and over again like conscious breathing, like meditating, like being and becoming, from the 10% towards the horizon.

*The more open the heart the smarter, brighter one becomes.*

What you put your attention on you energize and grow. What you send the conscious care of attention, breath and heart with invocation and ceremony to, you bring forward into life, as beauty in synergy with fluidity. Take a moment, have a moment, receive a moment and be, in Synergistic Fluidity.

## Diamond Heart Energy Activations
## STEP 8: DNA Essential Program Downloads
# Self Maintenance, Filtration and Protection

**AFFIRMATION:**

*I AM a Being of Violet Fire*

*I AM the Purity God Desires*

**ESSENTIAL PROGRAM #8 DESCRIPTION:**

Lucky we are, where, when and how, that grace has a place and a hope for us, that we may unfold the greatest good and support a world of grand design, not of our own making but divine and celestial. To begin to give birth to one's noble self and "observe that transformation", while taking note of the protection that, but not for its presence, planets would collide and the whole galaxy tumble into ruin. This is the beginning of peace. The end result of the cultivation of power and protection must be peace, and peace for everyone!

We have been told that even the corrupted atom can never surrender—except for the smallest aspect—to shadow and corruption, and that the center is always the uncorrupted liquid light of the One substance, and golden. Time and space can lend a mark but they cannot leave it. And Lucifer himself will be shown the door when the polarity game is complete.

But right now we are in the middle of it.

We need to have in place a shield that will work at the deepest levels and in the dark. We need to have established in our interior a smooth running forgiveness mechanism, an auto-pilot of welcoming compassion, a gear shift that reverses negativity, and gauges that measure the toxicity of place or situation and makes all the necessary adjustments of speed and direction, at the speed of light and the direction of right action, awareness and intention.

This Essential Program download brings this shining and redefining mechanism. It is the mind of the Buddha and the heart of the living Christ. It is a place in us where bad dreams go to die. It is the knowledge in us that watches as one's personal illusions go to the sacred fire. It is the ring of power and the emerald shield of protection. It is the courage that gives birth to love and the purity that unwinds the treads of fear and disillusion. It is the gift of the Violet Flame and the beginning of the dispensation of the new age that is upon many. It is a key for personal integrity and the way to live in the presence of unconditional love. This is the gift and responsibility.

Now, as we re-cap our phases of activation, we invoke these Essential Programs. First, we *Aligned the Trinity*. Second, we *Activated the Heart* and the three-fold flame of Love, Wisdom and Power. Third, we expanded our *Communication* network by expanding consciousness and making a determination that we are (can be) guided by the inner plane master teachers and angels. Fourth, we activated the program and DNA sequence for *Co-Creation and Creativity*. The Fifth program and activation focused our *Personal Covenants and the Divine Plan* and in the Sixth phase we became more Integrated with *Levels of Consciousness*. Now at the Seventh phase, we enter into *Smooth Running*, effortless adjusting and more masterful action and responses. The number 8 is the symbol of infinity. We can launch into a reaction-based reality or reach for the golden essence of our immortality, now in this moment. It is just a choice.

## Affirmations

*I AM a Being of Violet Fire*

*I AM the purity God desires.*

(Alternate these and weave them into the affirmations below)

*I AM a Violet Flame of unconditional love.*

*I AM a Violet Flame of transforming light.*

*I AM enveloped in a force field of infinite protection, which prevents anything that is not of the light from distracting me.*

*I AM the Beloved I AM Presence, invoking the full power of the Violet Flame to transmute cause, core, effect, record, and memory of all mis-qualified energy.*

*I AM directing a bundle of energy to spiral through all body levels, at all frequencies, in all dimensions, in all incarnations, in all realities, in all time frames to clear a path to unconditional love for all life.*

*I AM invoking a rainbow bridge of color and healing for my seven chakras and receiving this energy now.*

*I AM invoking the balance and harmony of the five elements of Fire, Water, Air, Earth and Etheric as protection and extension from subtle body to more subtle and spiritual until I AM whole, ascended and free.*

*I AM calling upon the Blue Sword of Michael the Archangel and his legions of light to cut me free, cut me free, cut me free.*

## Meditation

The *I AM* Meditation on Track 2 of Activation #8 MP3 follows here.

## Meditations on the Virtues of the Diamond Heart

## #8

## Self Awareness

## Self Maintenance, Filtration and Protection

Affirmation: *I AM a Being of Violet Fire*

Our synthesis of Maintenance, Filtration and Protection brings us to the appreciation of Self-Awareness. Emphasis on the Self here is a pivotal aspect of being. Most beings are unaware of the vital energies often lost because of cords, attachments, intrusions of questionable psychic forces, chakra imbalances, programs, trauma imprints, spiritual issues, cellular memory, curses, contracts, past life vows such as poverty, chastity and obedience, and of other soul programs. A psychologist visiting my practice was informed that someone had made a curse that was affecting her life. She responded that she knew exactly who it was. We cleared it. Another client was deeply drained by attending to a dying relative who had corded her. She was hospitalized with nothing wrong with her. Sadly I knew a young women who died of cancer in her twenties. She worked in a cancer facility. She had no business being there, period. Another time, I was corded by a bodywork client and had back pain for at least 12 hours following the session.

When people and systems break down, it is sometimes easy to see the contributing factors—sometimes. When people and systems run in harmony and balance it may require a leap of faith to accept the good favor. John Travolta said if Marilyn Monroe practiced Scientology she would be alive today...Who knows? I know that Jerry Seinfeld practices Transcendental Meditation and I never read about him driving one of his BMW's up a tree high on cocaine and alcohol; he meditates twice a day. I Meditate. I Clear. I use the Violet Flame, And you can too. Let's try this together.

Take a breath and relax a moment

*Beloved Mighty I AM Presence, Great Hosts of Ascended Masters, Mighty Legions of Light, Great Angelic Host, Great Cosmic beings and Great Cosmic Light, And All who govern the activities of the Sacred Fire to this Earth*

*Come, Come, Come in your Visible, Tangible, Ascended Master Bodies. Raise your Cosmic Blue Swords of Blue Flame of a Thousand Suns from the Great Central Sun, that transcends every human concept, quality or condition, and establish the Cosmic Sword of Blue Flame, the Spinning Violet Consuming Flame, and a Tornado of Blue Lightening of Divine Love from the Great Central Sun. In, through, and around us; and to every place, condition and thing associated with us in any way, and keep it in     constant action. Annihilate, annihilate, annihilate all that is not of the light in one mighty stroke! Send all these shadows back to the light for redefining, realigning or re-inspiring before these energies move out, in any way, again.*

*Release cause, effect, record and memory to energize our victory*

*To the Glory of the One and ALL*

*Take another breath*

*Let Go*

# Petals

*The blueprint for a Flower of a Thousand Petals*
*Sits upon your head.*
*Remember to care for this.*
*If weeds or tumble should banter here and around,*
*Be sure to uproot all of this.*
*Your heart know the secrets that make a flower bloom.*
*Listen to this silence at these morning dawns.*
*When faint lights born upon a sky so new,*
*Messages of light will stream into you . . .*
*Before the busy wandering day a moment's reflection,*
*Of the dreams that boldly guide your humble way.*
*Invite a warm recollection.*
*For hidden well springs in and of the soul,*
*Are not obtained in the market place.*
*And many a man's journey has torn him from home,*
*When easy enough he might have passed on it.*
*Know in this silence what most folks will not ever dare.*

*Be glad that you have had time*
*to become self aware.*
*Am I speaking to you and are you listening?*
*Pass beyond the time and mind of meaningless things,*
*Into a star lighted wind speeds resound.*
*I AM and I know just where I AM to go and exactly*
*just where I AM bound.*
*If still only a hint of this.*
*Consciousness becomes itself,*
*At the simple cost of presence.*
*Nothing binds me to become,*
*I AM free in all of my wanderings.*
*To dare to see my creations,*
*of silk of satin of stone and bone,*
*Self awareness becomes me.*

SELF Awareness is the meditation and virtue is the result of a Diamond Heart.

Diamond Heart Energy Activations
STEP NINE: DNA Essential Program Downloads

# Grounded in Awareness

## True liberation, expression and freedom are the result of "Awareness" which is your protection and power.

**AFFIRMATION:**

*I AM the Balance and Harmony God desires on this Earth right now.*

**ESSENTIAL PROGRAM #9 DESCRIPTION:**

When I was a child, I spoke as a child, thought like a child and acted like a child, and that was then. Now, *I AM* initiating a flow of energy activation as supervised by my *I AM* Presence, my holy Christed self and the Collective *I AM* Presence, for the expressed purpose of understanding why *I AM* here on Earth, and how to get around as best as I can, in balance and in harmony. This specific activation works by establishing a connection with my self, my body and the environment.

Our bodies are designed to work with tremendous sensitivity to changes in weather, as well as having abilities to recognize energy vortexes for the purpose of recharging.

You can take the sick to places or vortexes where miracles can happen through a natural re-polarization. You can change the placements of objects in locations and bring about tremendous energy upgrades. You will begin to understand and appreciate the application of color to your environment to bring out the best qualities. You can begin to appreciate with greater awareness and appreciation the use of crystals and herbs just by tuning in through your expanded and natural capacity. We are turning on a greater amount of brain capacity by invoking the superconscious supersensors. You are being wholly, newly hot-wired because we live in a universe of Ask, Seek and Knock and we are doing just that. We are asking for this specific upgrade to be downloaded into your circuits because it can, it will and it wants to assist you in every possible way to help you fulfill yourself in a fulfilling universe.

Trust your intuition. Trust your knowing. Trust your feeling. Be bold, be brave, and be innovative and original. Get ready for the wild, the wonderful and the never expected. You are preparing yourself to do here on earth, what you have come here to do. You are preparing yourself to be all you can be in light of the fact that every day you are evolving and becoming more and more capable of mastery. Your new spiral of energy/intention/surrender will transform misery into mastery.

*I AM* able to dream. *I AM* ready to dream. *I AM* willing to dream, and from this dream *I AM* bringing the focus, energy, determination to take it to the next level, then the next level, then the next level and so on and so on. Now, the past is just that and *I AM* allowing the sun and the Earth to open me to energies beyond any expectation I had as a child. Yesterday, I was my parent's child. Today, *I AM* a SUN/son or SUN/daughter of the highest, most auspicious and One Being, with access to whatever it is on this planet I need to begin to transform and transcend, to express and to prosper. *I AM* the balance and the harmony that I want and need; that the planet wants and needs; that the universe wants and needs. Today, right here and now, *I AM* accepting of this gift of life, this planetary awareness, this alignment with life, so that I may bodily, beautifully, boundlessly carry on with the business of being.

Now, we will re-cap our phases of activation as an invocation of these programs.

First, we invoke the *Alignment of the Harmonized Trinity*.

Second, we *Invoke the Activated Heart* and the three-fold flame of Love, Wisdom and Power.

Third, we invoke our communication network by expanding consciousness and making a determination that we are (can be) guided.

Fourth, we invoke the activation program and DNA sequence for *Co-Creation and Creativity*.

Fifth, we invoke the program and activation, which focuses our *Personal Covenants and the Divine Plan*.

Sixth, we invoke the *Integration of Levels of Multidimensional Consciousness*.

Seventh, we invoke and enter into *Smooth Running*, effortless adjusting and more masterful action and responses. The number 8 is the symbol of eternity/infinity.

Eighth, we can launch into a response-based reality and reach for the golden essence of our *Immortality*—now in this moment. It is just a choice.

This Ninth step, or essential program, is about opening one's eyes and truly seeing what is possible in spite of the odds. Now we are bending time or slowing it down by our breath. Our intentions warp the fabric of space to mold to our need because we hold to the decree of Right Action, Right Conduct and Right Intention. Accept this gift; you have worked hard to be here and will work even harder to expand and fulfill. *I AM* a being in balance and harmony with the laws of the universe and I create, I move, I think and I act, I respond and I Imagine in order, in rhythm, in beauty because I am in partnership with God. Right now, I belong on this planet because *I AM* here. My feet feel the pulse of the planet, the magnetic field. I am strapped in and ready to go.

**AFFIRMATIONS:**

*I AM here and now ready, willing and able.*

*I AM a Being of creativity and imagination.*

*Through me God's light pours forth into my creations.*

*I AM accepting the guidance flowing through me from spirit gratefully.*

*I AM magnetizing positive energy all around myself.*

*I AM radiating all positive energy into my environment.*

*I AM sustaining a positive energy disposition.*

***Affirmation: I AM the Balance and Harmony God desires on this Earth right now, grounded in awareness.***

**MEDITATION**

The *I AM* Meditation on Track 2 of Activation #9 MP3 follows here.

## Meditations on the Virtues of the Diamond Heart

## #9

# Grounded in Awareness

## True liberation, expression and freedom are the result of "Being Grounded in Awareness" which is your protection and power.

*Affirmation: I AM the Balance and Harmony God desires
on this Earth right now.
I look forward with confidence to the perfect realization
of the Eternal splendor of the Limitless Life.*

Our meditation here in this step number nine is the power of the three times three. The number nine is the number for completion. A certain cycle has been completed—but not everything. Being self aware, we become sensitive to the subtle forces that can get inside our field and influence our ability to express our talents and creations. Now another level, another consideration, another piece of the puzzle. We have the opportunity to be in touch with our OWN physical, mental, emotional and etheric nature and begin to energize and assimilate. We are absorbing the finer energies from the sun in our food, in our environment. We begin to send out our own light rays before us to illumine the path. We become solution oriented. Many of our associates, family and friends are not moving at our speed and wish to engage us in their drama. Why? Misery loves company. We are only available to a solution consciousness. We have made the distinction. We are becoming more and more grounded in awareness as a fact of our lives.

Years ago people had some interesting ideas about ascension. Quite a few people thought when the Hale Bopp comet passed this way it was going to pick up some hitchhikers. One might consider this possibility of resonance. That is when the four lower bodies of physical, mental, emotional and etheric have been returned to their pristine probabilities and possibilities, free of karma and horizontal or earthbound tendencies; a natural realignment with source and light emerges.

You see we collectively created a need for Jesus when we had mistaken the Door to Freedom as a door to persecution. Guilt, a false virtue will do this. We could not see the door for what was, is and will be, an open invitation to recall, to renew, to become aware again and to become grounded in awareness. This is the only reason we require any outside assistance, because we have pulled a bag over our own heads and now often only see the phantoms of our ideas and projections through our guilt filters. We are not good enough for God so reversely God is not good enough for us—a strange but popular mental occupation. Release yourself by bringing the light of love, of truth, of possibility, into the four lower bodies. Lighten up. If it were not for us, Jesus would not be that great. We fall and he calls and all is right as rain again. Stay grounded. Stay grounded in awareness.

## To Ground Myself in Awareness

*I call upon the Light for myself and all Sentient Beings,*
*Please Ground us in Awareness.*
*I call up the Violet Flame of Unconditional Love,*
*Please Ground us in Forgiveness.*
*I call upon the Ascension Flame to Radiate us Free,*
*Please Ground us in this Bliss.*
*I call upon the Flame of the Immaculate Concept,*

*Please Ground Us in this Real*
*Peace of Existence.*

*I was a tiny electron one day and dreamed of being an elemental,*
*I awoke as an elemental.*
*I was an elemental one day and dreamed of being a Rose,*
*I woke up as a Rose.*
*I was a Rose one day and dreamed of flying like an Eagle,*
*I woke up flying like an Eagle.*
*I was an Eagle one day and dreamed of being a Man.*
*I woke up one day as a Man.*
*I was a Man one day and dreamed of being a Star.*
*I woke up one day as a star.*
*I was a star one day and dreamed of being a Sun.*
*I woke up as the Sun.*
*I was a Sun that day when I woke up wondering*
*what I will dream of next.*
*A God?*
*God only knows*
*Light shall unfold Us*
*Arise the trumpets sound off*
*Remember to Be and with consistency*
*Stay grounded in Awareness.*

(This meditation on the virtue of the Diamond Heart is *I AM* grounded in awareness)

## Diamond Heart Energy Activations
### STEP 10: DNA Essential Program Downloads
# Peace • Power • Prosperity

**AFFIRMATION:**

*I AM manifesting all that I need,
all that I want and all that I desire.*

**ESSENTIAL PROGRAM #10 DESCRIPTION:**

There is a saying in the martial arts that if you want to move quickly, practice moving slowly, if you want to move like lightening then practice standing still. In this energy packet and receptor we have a trinity of words to describe the Ready – Aim – Fire quality of this program. And as if entering into the Stillness of All Possibility, we do access the cosmic bank of stored energy in the causal realm, to bring forward that which we need, want and desire to have manifest. As the Master Jesus told us, "It is your Father's good pleasure to give you the Kingdom" and now we begin to reflect this in our Earthly lives.

We need to understand here, that it is not what we ask for that matters, it is what we ask *with*. It is not the strength of the outer personality but the lightening power of the "Mighty *I AM* Presence" that commands the action. The great universe does not only permit us to use the "*I AM* Presence" we are required to master the laws of this life and evolve to the next dimension. We want to access the peace that passes understanding, the power that moves and builds and creates in balance, beauty and harmony to manifest the prosperity that is ours to have and enjoy. Remember we all have a rich Father, and in the immortal words of the Upanishads we have this:

*"All this is full. All that is full. From fullness comes fullness and when fullness is taken from fullness, fullness remains."*

Remember, you can manifest a thing by first holding the thought (Ready), speaking the word (Aim), and acting in your own life (Fire). Now your presence releases to you, the life quality to bring this forward in peace, in power and prosperity. We make a call that is constructive that would never bring harm to any one.

Mighty *I AM* Presence here "*I AM*", "*I AM* ready", "*I AM* willing", and "*I AM* able" to go forth and do the perfect thing that is appropriate for me to do. Stop qualifying things in human terms and start re-qualifying them in terms of the "*I AM* Presence" which knows no lack or limitation whatsoever. The power that made this world and everything in it, is the power that made your body-mind-spirit so align, define and deliver on the need and want and desire.

Now I/we will recap our phases of activation as an invocation of these programs.

First, I/we invoke the *Alignment of the Harmonized Trinity*.

Second, we invoke the *Activated Heart* and the three-fold flame of Love, Wisdom and Power.

Third I/we invoke our *Communication network* of expanding consciousness and make a determination that we are (can be) guided.

Fourth, I/we invoke the activated program and DNA sequence for *Co-Creation and Creativity*.

Fifth, I/we invoke the program and activation which focuses our *Personal Covenants and the Divine Plan*.

Sixth, I/we invoke the integration of levels of *Multidimensional Consciousness*.

Seventh, I/we invoke and enter into *Smooth Running*, effortless adjusting and more masterful action and responses.

Eighth, I/we invoke a *Higher Response-Based Reality* and reach for the golden essence of the *I AM* Presence now in this moment. It is just a choice.

Ninth, I/we have established *Balance and Harmony* in the affairs of our life! I can create, I move, I think and I act, I respond and I imagine in order, in rhythm, in beauty because *I AM* in partnership with God. Right now I belong on this planet because *I AM* here. My feet feel the pulse of the planet, the magnetic field. I am strapped in and ready to go.

Now in this Tenth Step, we can focus and manifest through presenting ourselves in peace, in power, in prosperity. Each activation is a turn of the wheel and a step closer to our goal of being co-creators with the One Being.

## Affirmations:

*I Am the Presence of Peace.*

*I AM the Presence of Power on Purpose.*

*I AM the Fulfillment of Prosperity.*

*I AM A Manifesting co-creator capable of magic and wonder.*

*I AM aligned with the Presence of supply.*

*I AM the action of focus, of love and intuition.*

*I AM the ability to Ready, to Aim and to Fire spirit inspired creations that brings reward responsibly to my life.*

*I AM the Presence of Love for the Creator, creating my gifts of appreciation in all areas of my life.*

*I AM the Spirit of Peace, the Presence of Power and the magnificence of manifestation for unfolding my destiny and purpose unencumbered.*

*I AM surrendered to allowing the flow of the universe to peacefully, powerfully and prosperously manifest through and around me now and forever!*

*I AM manifesting all that I need, all that I want and all that I desire!*

## Meditation

The *I AM* Meditation on Track 2 of Activation #10 MP3 follows here.

## Meditations on the Virtues of the Diamond Heart
## #10
## Peace • Power • Prosperity

Affirmation: *I AM Manifesting all that I need, all that I want and all that I desire.
In Thought, Word and Deed I rest my life upon the shore foundation of Eternal being.*

*"All this is full. All that is full. From fullness comes fullness and when fullness is taken from fullness, fullness remains".*   The Upanishads

As we enter into this tenth meditation *I AM* energized by all the triple complex of words that once again define our virtue, peace, power and prosperity. I can tell you that I have read a lot abut how prosperity can take a load off your mind, give you peace and that is powerful. I have noticed that people who have truly stood for peace are very powerful. People, such as the Dali Lama, who can forgive others for grievous errors committed against them or their people are powerful in peaceful ways. One also has to acknowledge the power of people like Bill Gates, who has generously set out about the safe and productive return of money to the public, such that other billionaires are throwing money at his cause. That is the power of prosperity seeking the peace of balance and harmony with people. I think we might also acknowledge President Barack Obama for donating his winnings from his Nobel Peace prize to charity. Headlines might read, Peace Prize Powers Prosperity for People. Pretty good.

## Returning

*I AM returning to where I must be,*

*in peace, in power in prosperity*

*The thought, the word the action,*

*The body the mind the spirit unified*

*Aligning courage, confidence and surrender*
*at once a simple and fluid gentle motion,*
*Now a wave of spiraling light and sound.*
*Of power of love and of wisdom,*
*Of peace and equanimity,*
*Of prosperity too.*
*And any knowledge the ancestors bring to give,*
*Have ancient roots in a hidden father time.*
*Our channel opens,*
*Communication, Transformation, Transmutation.*
*A wonderful Tube of White Light all around you,*
*One Mind, One Self, One Purpose.*
*Sharing Pulses of Presence with Charm,*
*Co-Creation, Talents and Productivity.*
*Sharing Pulses of Presence divine,*
*A Covenant of Life, a Purpose and Plan,*
*An intimate compelling commending peace stand.*

*Enough to Be Still,*
*To Know, To dare and To be Silent.*
*Flow into In a deep Oneness of things.*
*Nothing but this to satisfy a deep settled soul's pursuit.*
*Organization, Cooperation renders momentum,*
*Of beauty, of balance, of dreams*
*Synergy, Fluidity and Beauty*
*Ready to Fire this Aim.*
*Sacred Fire Love that flows from above,*
*A total and all embracing victory,*
*Our one and encompassing desire.*

*Remember that Peace flows out of Awareness.*

*Ground yourself in the Ascension/ Resurrection Flame of Love.*

*A Rainbow bridge for your feet to dance upon, heard far oft,*

*A distant sound of trumpet, and this tunes the crystalline clean air.*

*When a Peace that passeth all understanding,*

*Embraces you comfortably tight and so right,*

*You'll sense a fragrance of powers of prosperity flowing,*

*A crystal river running off to a deep and a wondrous sea.*

*A wide mouthed Blue Opal Open Ocean Smiles,*

*I AM returning to where I must be.*

*Peacefully, Prosperously and Powerfully,*

*I AM Returning to where I must be.*

*In Thought, Word and Deed,*

*I rest my life, my body, my mind and spirit, this unity,*

*upon this shore foundation of eternal being.*

*I AM returning to where I must be.*

After liberating yourself of the expectations placed upon you by your parents, peers, television and by your culture and community,

*Free yourself of the expectations you have falsely placed upon yourself.*
*Then you can love yourself FREE*

*I AM manifesting all that I need, all that I want and all that I desire,*

*Now reads I AM manifesting all that I truly need,*

*all that I truly want and all that I truly desire,*

*In Peace, In Power, In Prosperity*

*for me to be Free*

*Allowing the seasons to guide us*

*Following a lightness of touch*

*Releasing any hold that might bind us*

*Increasing humble surrender, thus*

*Focusing freedom for peace*

*Into a new and higher ethic*

*Where a divine wind fills sails*

*Into a new and higher ethic*

*Where a divine will prevails.*

*What is a divine will?*

*That which knows no opposition, limitation or chance. It is a fulcrum of infinite light!*

*We apologize for any confusion*

*And we just want to give you a shout*

*You have been living your life from outside in it seems*

*You had better turn yourself Inside out*

*Being Source*

*Directed and Sustained*

Silence: for a moment let this Peace come to visit with you!

# Diamond Heart Energy Activations
## STEP 11: DNA Essential Program Downloads
# A Waking Dream

**AFFIRMATION:**

*I AM Awake in Life*
*my Dreams I do recall*

The Tao is the source of the ten thousand things. It is the home of the good man and the refuge for the bad. Sweet words can't buy honor. Good deeds will bring respect. If a man is not good yet do not neglect him, remain still and offer a gift of the Tao. Why does everybody like the Tao so much? It is because you receive what you want and what you need, and come to a state of balance after trying and failing, so much so often. Here in this moment another gift, another breath, another possibility, another dream. Until you are fully awakened, may you be blessed to have real nice dreams and to remember them as well!

**ESSENTIAL PROGRAM #11 DESCRIPTION:**

In the East there are four unique states of mind defined by psychologists, the master's and yogi's: waking, sleeping, dreaming and meditating. Someone asked the Buddha if he slept or not; he said that the body goes to sleep but for him "awareness is always happening". The ability to recall one's dreams can be of most important assistance to the unfolding and awakening individual. The higher self communicates this way to the conscious mind, when messages go unheard, so dreams can direct us. Dreams release energy and stress. Until there are no more dreams and only awareness, only the flow of all connected things moving upon the screen of consciousness, we need to honor the dream. We need to be able to remember it and interpret it properly. We need to be empowered by it. We need to dream the dream of dreams and be connected.

This activation gives us this access and allows a more potent participation in this aspect of consciousness. By affirming *"I AM awake in life my dreams I do recall"* we get in close and personal to the dream. You may want to keep some writing materials near your bed. Your first 60 seconds of waking state are golden—this is the time you must access your dream state. Once you start planning your day, the dream state recedes into the background.

If you wake up during the night, focus your attention on the inner levels and allow your dreams to come to the surface. You want to affirm discretion by knowing which dreams are worth giving attention to or not. The dream experts say that we all use universal images and symbols that are rich in meaning and that these dreams may unlock precious new and emerging resources within our psych. If you have a bad dream, do not give it any energy as 99% of the times it is your body/mind simply releasing stress, records and memory!

As we flow through the language and imagery invoked by the etheric templates of each session, we begin to see the tapestry of being, the color of our consciousness; we hear the sound of our spark and gaze into the light of our spirit. We sleep and dream and awaken to a new and unified consciousness that moves towards the Tao, towards the One, towards the light.

First I dreamt in the dark and now I dream in the light of understanding until at last I dream no more. I will sit with the Buddha one day and dream no more.

As we invoke the progression of activations allow yourself to feel as if you are being wrapped in the petals of possibility of the Lotus of True Being.

First, I/we invoke the *Alignment of the Harmonized Trinity*.

Second, I/ we invoke the *Activated Heart* and the three-fold flame of Love, Wisdom and Power.

Third, I/we invoke our *Communication* network of expanding consciousness and make a determination that we are (can be) guided.

Fourth, I/we invoke the activated program and DNA sequence for *Co-Creation and Creativity*.

Fifth, I/we invoke the program and activation which focuses our *Personal Covenants and the Divine Plan*.

Sixth, I/we invoke the Integration of *Levels of Multidimensional Consciousness*.

Seventh, I/we invoke and enter into *Smooth Running*, effortless adjusting and more masterful action and responses.

Eighth, I/we invoke a higher response-based reality and reach for the golden essence of the *I AM* Presence now in this moment. It is just my choice.

Ninth, I/we have established *Balance and Harmony* in the affairs of our life! I can create, I move, I think and I act, I respond and I imagine in order, in rhythm, in beauty because I am in partnership with God. Right now I belong on this planet because *I AM* here. My feet feel the pulse of the planet, the magnetic field.

Tenth, I/we can *Focus and Manifest Through Presence*, allowing for peace, in power in prosperity. Each activation is a turn of the wheel and a step closer to our goal of being co-creators with the One Being.

AFFIRMATIONS:

*I AM Awake in life
and my dreams I do recall.*

(Use the above affirmation as soon as you wake up.)

*I AM a being of power, imagination whose dreams come true.*

*I AM an expression of the creativity of having dreamed with the One Being.*

*I AM an avenue for my dreams to walk and enrich my community.*

*I AM filled with the appreciation of the dream coming true.*

*I AM tapped into the cosmic dream factory.*

*I AM able to drift through states of sleep, dream, awake and meditation as a flow of presence, awareness and peace, as a unified field of consciousness.*

*I AM dreaming the dream, awake to beauty and boundlessness.*

*I AM living, moving from this creative spiritual center where my dreams align with the creative endeavors of all sentient beings.*

*I AM looking forward to the crystal clear dreams that inform and enlighten me. I rest in peace. I dream in Kaleidoscope color and beauty.*

*I AM touching the living pulsing light of dreamtime to take me beyond space, beyond time, beyond form, beyond mind into the wonder of opaque silent stillness.*

*I AM an actor in the eternal dream of living light.*

***I AM Awake in my life***
***my dreams I do recall.***

## MEDITATION

The *I AM* Meditation on Track 2 of Activation # 11 MP3 follows here.

## Meditations on the Virtues of the Diamond Heart
## #11
## A Waking Dream

Affirmations: *I AM Awake in Life my dreams I do recall.*

*The Kingdom of the Spirit is embodied in my flesh.*

*Continuity is a Virtue: A flow of meditation, dreaming,*

*waking and sleeping.*

Beginning with a meditation on the value and virtue of meditation is very Zen, to say the least. Chop that wood, carry water, hey what's the sound of one hand clapping? Continuity of what? Continuity of consciousness, of course. Who is to say one is not asleep when they are waking? Look around. If dreaming is a way to render messages to the conscious mind that it has been too busy to hear or recognize, then how can we say we are dreaming, and not communicating? If thinking happens when *I AM* meditating then am I really meditating? What about beta levels, alpha levels, theta levels and delta? Sleeping at a beta level might seem like a bad dream to some, but soldiers in hot spots or ninjas train for this and can stay alive by it. Stay alert!

Also, a trained professional dowser (pendulum researcher) can enter into a delta brain wave pattern that will totally challenge any technician. They are seeing brain waves similar to people that are in a coma. Remember the Buddha said, "The body sleeps but awareness always is the case". He may have said continuity is always the case, but he was past the dreaming stage, no need. Last night I dreamed I was in a mildly heated debate with my father. He died 10 years ago. This morning I asked myself, "What is the one thing I would say to him if he were alive today?" I decided it was "Thank you"!

Another day, another clearing, another cup of coffee and, today I will dress for success, and dream my way! I recently received word about a young man who was off his game—stress, substance, relationship and money. He listened to the 12 minute *I AM* meditation CD, (Tract 2 on the activations CD) for 30 days in a row and his whole life shifted. This was the word that came back to us. He lives, he loves, he laughs and somehow continuity returned. In almost every human endeavor there is a training for doing, this, that or the other thing—sports, the arts, science. This is a training for being. Remember to just say "thank you" and stay alert!

Commit to 12 minutes of *I AM* meditation for 40 days and see the results.

# A Welcoming Dream

*No such thing as arriving when you are already here, there.*
*I wonder now from time to time, sometimes at stars I stare.*
*So much time, so much space and so much mystery,*
*I stare into the bright future, behind me fading history.*
*Now dream time happens between the lines sometimes.*
*A ferris wheel-like movement of color and passion,*
*I dream about all the sea shells that as a child I found,*
*Ocean waves gently rocking my boat of innocence and emotion.*
*Right by the sea, every day the sun, right out of her would rise.*
*Then my dreaming would stop most abruptly, right before my eyes.*
*I wonder what a bear dreams about, way out there in the wild,*
*Or birds that climb upon sky, that still sleep in the trees.*
*The wise old owl stays up all night and must rest his own way*
*No dreams at all will be installed if sleeping is by day.*
*Should a child dream about the future or about their wondrous ways?*
*The lover spoiled by dreams gone south has yet another play.*

*The banker's dreams are heavy so much change to carry round.*
*A poet dreams as light as feathers shaping every sound.*
*The painter has a color for every dream that he has turned.*
*The worker has a vision for every dollar earned.*
*The lover dreams of allowance for roses, candles, wine.*
*The mother has to cover the expenses for her child.*
*So much color so much structure so much movement moving forth,*
*I wonder where to place this care and dream power being born.*
*If thoughts are things and magnetize rings of probability and fate,*
*Dreams must have life, must have light on toward a heavenly state.*

*To these high peaked mountain dreams,*

*To these deep blue ocean's dreams too.*

*To this dream voice that guides the soul of a man,*

*To these dreams we wish come true.*

*To these dreams that shape a country,*

*To these dreams that shape a man.*

*There is no dream to dream at all, or brighter to understand.*

*The is no brighter dream to dream at all*

*Beyond the great " I AM".*

*So much of there, here.*

*So much color, so much structure, so much movement, moving forth*

*I wonder where to place this care and dream power being born.*

*Ok, if thoughts are things, dreams can be too, ok come on in.*

*If you pray in times of distress and in need, then for balance sake,*

*at least dream in ecstasy and abundance.*

*I AM Awake in life my dreams I do recall.*

*I AM Awake in life my dreams I do unfold.*

*I AM Awake in life my dreams I do install.*

*I AM Awake in Life My dreams I do in bold.*

Diamond Heart Energy Activations
Step 12--DNA Essential Program Downloads

# Returning Point
# The Octave
# Angel Eyes

**AFFIRMATION:**

*I AM accessing the gifts of my past and possibilities of my future with the light of wisdom.*

**ESSENTIAL PROGRAM #12 DESCRIPTION:**

Power alone is a blind force. Love alone lacks the potency of discretion but wisdom and power and love are the gifts of the Creator and are bestowed upon the precious few who work for them and eventually earn them. *Arate'* is a Greek word that describes the true alignment of the body, mind and spirit. *Arate'* was a female contemporary of Socrates. The daughter of Aristoppos and considered to possess the splendor of Greece, the beauty of Helen, with the virtue of Thirma, the pen of Aristippos, the soul of Socrates and the tongue of Homer. *Arete'* from the same root means the goodness, virtue and excellence to which we all aspire to achieve.

Wisdom and power walk hand in hand; without both, either is useless and non-existent, for power is not created without wisdom and wisdom is only attained through development and the use of power. (*The Emerald Tablets*)

Now, an access to the higher principles of life is awakening within you.

This is the way of the Tao and now this is your way. One cannot be expected to see in the dark without the light of the Self. The light is on in you and your knowing to call upon the presence is well established.

In a chromatic scale in music, the $12^{th}$ note is the octave and keynote. In the Tarot, the Hanged Man is the $12^{th}$ card and the meaning for this is the "suspended mind" or the total and utter dependence of the human personality upon the cosmic life. Water is the element associated with *"Mem"*, the $12^{th}$ letter in the Hebrew alphabet. Water reflects images and was the first mirror. Water is considered the mother to all minerals and living things consist of minerals, or elements.

Congratulations! You have traveled far and will travel now, even further in the unfolding of your destiny and unraveling of the mystery of the Self, and of the universe of which you are taking part. This is a free will zone. This is a field of action and reaction. There are laws that govern everything. All of the circumstances of your life are the result of past actions, past deeds and dreams fulfilled, or left for tomorrow to be fulfilled. You are a galactic citizen. You are a multi-dimensional being. You have access to the causal body and can reel in the energies from all your good deeds of the past. You have a cosmic bank account and you have access to the "Book of Life", perhaps through dreams or meditations or a pure sense of intuition. Now you have arrived at the other shore and are no longer the babe in the woods, but a son/daughter of the Most High.

Most traditions offer at birth a sacrament such as baptism; and in the adolescent phase a confirmation. This is your rite of initiation, your rite of passage. Now you may call upon the Mighty *I AM* Presence and receive the guidance that you need to move in all directions. Much light has been given and many new doors are opening to new and exciting realities and possibilities. The old skin has been sloughed off and a new skin emerges with new desires, new awareness and new potential. Because you have invoked the progression of activations to allow yourself to emerge like a statue cut from stone, like the wood carved with skill and patience, or the diamond once rough, but that now shines. We complete this cycle and reach the keynote and the octave of our own personal symphony of being. We vibrate a new light and tone because we have taken the spiral stairway as follows:

First, I/we invoke the *Alignment of the Harmonized Trinity*.

Second, I/ we invoke the *Activated Heart* and the three-fold flame of Love, Wisdom and Power.

Third, I/we invoke our *Communication* network of expanding consciousness and make a determination that we are guided.

Fourth, I/we invoke the activated program and DNA sequence for *Co-Creation and Creativity*.

Fifth, I/we invoke the program and activation, which focuses our *Personal Covenants and the Divine Plan*.

Sixth, I/we invoke the integration of levels of *Multidimensional Consciousness*.

Seventh, I/we invoke and enter into *Smooth Running*, effortless adjusting and more masterful action and responses.

Eighth, I/we invoke a higher response-based reality and reach for the *Golden Essence of the I AM Presence*, now in this moment. It is just my choice.

Ninth, I/we establish *Balance and Harmony* in the affairs of our life! I can create, I move, I think and I act, I respond and I imagine in order, in rhythm, in beauty because I am in partnership with God. Right now, I belong on this planet because *I AM* here. My feet feel the pulse of the planet, the magnetic field.

Tenth, I/we focus and manifest through presence, allowing for *Peace, in Power in Prosperity*. Each activation is a turn of the wheel and a step closer to our goal of being co-creators with the One Being.

Eleventh, I/we invoke the *Continuity of Consciousness* by affirming "*I AM* awake in life and my dreams I do recall".

Now, at the 12th step we call upon the law of life and ask for the Seal of Solomon, for the Star of David, for the Ascended Master Consciousness, for the mind of the Buddha and the heart of the living Christ, for the Diamond Heart, for the Ancient Eyes and for as much light as we are capable of receiving to pour forth upon us at this time, to allow us to arrive at this next dimension or level of ourselves in God's most Holy Name.

AFFIRMATIONS:

*I AM the Resurrection and the Life, Body Maintenance and Alignment of the Trinity of Being.*

*I AM Multidimensional Communications.*

*I AM Being Divinely Guided.*

*I AM a magical being of infinite creativity.*

*I AM unfolding my covenants and unfolding the divine plan.*

*I AM RE-defining RE-developing and RE-directing my personal database to be in alignment with my higher self.*

*I AM up regulating, up grading automatically.*

*I Am a Being of Violet Fire.*

*I AM the Balance and Harmony God desires on Earth, right now.*

*I AM manifesting all that I need, want and desire.*

*I AM awake in life, my dreams I recall.*

*I AM accessing my gifts developed in the past.*

## OPTIONAL READING

*I AM accessing energies of the union of two triangles of fire and water, the Star of David and my Merkaba of protection.*

*I AM protected by the Light of Wisdom and of Truth.*

*I AM unfolding my destiny as directed and decided.*

*I AM invincible and invulnerable to mis-direction.*

*I AM a being of substance and honor directing great energy.*

*I AM an open channel for expression of harmony and beauty in all my affairs and in all my creations.*

*I AM the realization of gratitude.*

*I AM That Mighty Beloved I AM Presence.*

### MEDITATION

The *I AM* Meditation on Track 2 on the Activation #12 MP3 follows here.

## Meditations on the Virtues of the Diamond Heart

## #12

## All the Power That Ever Was or Will be is Here Now

## Returning Point
## The Octave
## Angel Eyes

Affirmation: *I AM accessing the gifts of my past and possibilities of my future with the light of Wisdom.*

The Key note has once again been sung. This time it is the octave. We have completed our circle of 12, bringing the wisdom of experience to an attitude of enthusiasm and excitement to be where we are now, also ready to begin again. We are at the Returning Point of Light, the Solstice, the longest day of light and possibility. Congratulations and we sincerely wish that you will now be born again. We wish that the magical formulas have opened up in the etheric and that you will now start to go over them, share them and get to the next level.

The octave may also be seen as one's ability to stay present, in the now. As we enter into this exciting time on the planet we want to simply stay present and not move into the future or dwell on the past. We want to be all that we can be in a simple and supportive role for those around us. If we look horizontally at an octave, we see it across a page like CC#DD#EFF#GG#AA#BC. The activations are vertical and are beginning to take you from the 3rd dimension and 7 chakras to the 5th dimension as a Solar 12 chakra Being of Light who remembers to Co-Create with a higher power, through *I AM* Awareness. The octave is the POWER OF NOW!

Angel Eyes is the acknowledgment of the Beings of Light who have traveled before us and left their name and energy in the ethers around planet Earth. The Names of these beings strike a harmonic that warms the heart and re-focuses the spirit.

## A Poem for Those Bright, Enlightened Ones

*We acknowledge Abraham the Father of the Jews,*
*We acknowledge Moses and Joseph and Jesus too.*
*Gandhi was guided by a light from above while reading*
*the Bible, the Gita and the Koran.*
*Ramana Maharshi, Suzuki Zen Roshi, Rama Krishna*
*were bright shining stars,*
*Take a moment now to wonder just where they are,*
*They are with you.*
*Mary, Martha and Mother Theresa were women who tipped*
*the scales of the human mind from closed to openness.*
*The actions they took were blanketed in compassion and kindness,*
*They had the Angel Eyes.*
*Francis of Assisi, so simple and pure and he opened a door*
*for more to walk through.*
*Babaji has been walking around in India*
*for generations and generations,*
*He lives in a cave.*
*Lincoln was a great president and worked to free the slaves.*
*Confucius contributed to our thinking with his commentary*
*on the I Ching.*
*Rumi the master poet, where do we begin?*
*So many prophets go unnamed in time, also Elijah comes here to mind.*
*Matthew, Mark, John and Luke gave it all.*
*Lakshmi, Jove, Krishna, Kuan Yin and the Keeper of the Scrolls.*
*Messengers too, to us from the secret love stars.*
*Here is hope, here is love, here is joy, here the reason why,*
*We have come to recognize,*

the Angel Eyes.
Archangels Michael, Raphael, Gabriel, Ariel, Azrael,
Chamuel, Haniel, Jeremiel,
Jophiel, Metatron, Raguel, Raziel, Sandalphon, Uriel, Zadkiel.
We have all been graced by their wings.
St Germain, Sanat Kumara,
Saraswathi the Goddess,
And the great spirit of the Ascension Flame.
The Green Tara of healing, the White Tara of illumination,
Zarathustra and the Angels of the Sacred Fire,
Yogananda, Lao Tzu, Melchizedek and
the Brothers and Sisters of the Golden Robe too,
Welcome these Angel Eyes to open for you!
From the Point of Light within the mind of God,
Let Light pour forth into the minds of men,
Let Light descend on Earth.

All the Power that ever was or will be is here now.

# A Sun/Son/Daughter of Illumination

*Participate in the greatest show on Earth,*
*The arrival of your own Self, which finally comes down to greet you*
*As Transmutation's Violets Rays wash all over you.*
*A Divine Mother Pink, Heavenly Father Blue*
*An Ocean's wonder wave that washes your dreams,*
*Casually, joyfully comes and freely spirals through.*
*Celebrate so silk and softly through Enchanted Tones and Dance*
*Your Innocence flowering an Ancient Original Face.*
*The Sacred Fire Flame of the Original Concept blazes, always*
*For me and for you, After all, it is our time that's due, accept this.*
*So many mountains that I have seen, that you have climbed*
*And now One more Sun of Illumination rises up to delight you.*
*To Illumine your path your heart and your mind*
*Give in to a moment of Now, and of Wonder*
*Give in to a moment of Now, of This Sweet Sacred Fire Kiss.*
*Participate, Transmute, Celebrate, Illuminate*
*Be the gift of giving of living, Surrendered,*
*Participate, Transmute, Celebrate, Illuminate.*
*Be the gift of giving of living*
*Surrendered*
*To Only This One,*
*Sun of Illumination*

# APPENDIX I

# The Affirmations

The following affirmations define the intent and character of each of the sessions. The energy for each session is a causal/etheric energy template that activates the individuals requesting the activation. It is in essence a baptism of Sacred Fire from the octave of love, the octave above. The discipline of spiritual unfolding is the directing of Intention, the receptivity of *allowing* and the appreciation for *grace*.

1. **BODY ELEMENTAL—BODY AWARENESS—ALIGNMENT OF THE TRINITY:** *I AM the resurrection and the life of my body/mind and spirit.*

2. **COMMUNICATION:** *I AM multidimensional communications.*

3. **GUIDANCE AND INTUITION:** *I AM being divinely guided.*

4. **CO-CREATION, TALENTS, PRODUCTIVITY:** *I AM a magical being of infinite creativity.*

5. **COVENANTS, PURPOSE, PLAN:** *I AM unfolding my covenants and unfolding the divine plan.*

6. **ORGANIZATION AND CO OPERATION:** *I AM re-defining, re-developing and re-directing my personal database to be in alignment with my higher self.*

7. **SYNERGY AND FLUIDITY:** *I AM up-regulating, up-grading automatically.*

8. **SELF-MAINTENANCE, FILTRATION & PROTECTION:** *I Am a being of violet fire.*

9. **GROUNDED IN AWARENESS:** *I AM the balance and harmony God desires on Earth right now.*

10. **PEACE, POWER AND PROSPERITY:** *I AM manifesting all that I need, want and desire.*

11. **I DREAM WITH AWARENESS AND RECALL:** *I AM awake in life, my dreams I recall.*

12. **THE RETURNING POINT, THE OCTAVE, ANGEL EYES:** *I AM accessing my gifts developed in the past.*

# APPENDIX II

# Declaration of the Light

I have the inner light and strength to forgive myself for every emotion of anger and fear that I have gone through this past day, week, year and back as far as I can reach,

I forgive myself and everyone who may have offended me.

I will let go and forgive the universe and all its people and conditions that have pushed me to the dark side of myself.

I forgive myself for giving up on people who deserved more from me, who deserved a second chance, with more compassion and understanding.

I forgive all that have cast zingers at my heart, my dreams, my ideas and my soul.

Forgiveness is my healing balm, mentally I rub this on my heart and soul. Forgiveness is the tune I sing and the dance I move my feet to, also.

I forgive and become a living vortex of light and positive energy transforming myself through acceptance of what is. By accepting those people around me whom I have been challenged to understand fully, not knowing their unique place in God's unfolding universe.

I send this Statement of Forgiveness to the One and in return I am being set free, to be myself, liberated.

I shall not sweat the small stuff.

# APPENDIX III

# The Reset Exercise

Dear Anyone and/or Everyone,

If I have compromised you, or caused you harm, in any way possible, either for real or imagined, in this life or any other life, in this dimension or any other dimension, I humbly apologize to you. I ask for your complete forgiveness here and now.

And, I forgive you likewise.

Also I release myself from having to contribute to your well being in all ways unless you specifically ask. I am here to work on myself!

And, I release you likewise.

You are a great human being. We have the same Creator.

*I AM* perusing my destiny and completion with planet Earth and it's fine people. *I AM* returning home, in LIGHT fashion.

You are completely excused from having to either understand or appreciate what this means to ME.

There is no assessment or validation that you have to make about my decisions. You are free to move forward respectfully!

You may choose to ask God or not, what the plan for me is. I am in partnership with Her!

I am finished explaining myself! I am finished trying to explain myself!

*I AM* not a victim in any way shape or form. I accept responsibility for what I attract in my life; therefore, I reserve this right for myself and for you!

If I feel, intuit or observe in any way that you or any other person is compromised by blocks, blindness, cords, distortions, entities, karma, cooties, crap, time capsules, openings, spiral tracks, thought forms, trauma imprints, gas or any other condition: I reserve the right to head for the hills. I support OUR Freedom to Choose!

My moment of Now is Sacred and Self-sustaining. It has a future pull and so it does NOT require any traction from *any* past, whatever reality, idea, dream or nightmare it may be.

*I AM* a heart centered being of Light on Purpose, *I AM* sending out a blessing to all life! Not because (state your name) is, was, or will continue to be, but simply because, *I AM*.

*I AM* here and now re-setting my goals, practice and orientation for ALL my relationships. All cords are cut and, only heartstrings need apply.      Namáste!

# APPENDIX IV

# Re-Set / Namáste Exercise

After reading the Re-Set Exercise out loud the *Namáste* greeting brings more emotion to the surface, tears of joy and laughter of release.

We have experimented with going around the room and having each person who wishes to, to read a sentence of the Re-Set out loud. This charges the room with a larger than individual intent and promotes a group chemistry.

*Namáste is a greeting from heart to heart.*

*Namáste is the recognition that God stuff abides here.*

*Namáste transcends the flesh to the Spirit of Fellowship and the Heart of Belonging.*

*Namáste is this flow of a finer wave of the lightness of Being.*

Let each person who is present and who cares to participate, simply move around the room and do the *Namáste*, hands across the heart, blessing for one another.

Allow enough time for each person to *Namáste* all they like.

Allow time for integration.

Namáste

# APPENDIX V

# Standing Wave, Take 5
# Re-patterning your relationship with Gravity

It is the simplest of discoveries that have the greatest impact upon our lives. This morning I was reflecting on this as a possibility for this ultra simple exercise that has been named the "Standing Wave". By simply standing comfortably with feet 2 to 4 inches apart one initiates a movement from heal to toe and back again. The whole movement is limited to that. NO wobbles, No shakes, No moving of the arms but instead just relaxing ANY AND ALL muscles that are not directly involved.

This is the progression of awareness as we move slowly back and forth as a Standing Wave, heel to toe, feet planted solid on the ground.

1. Make sure you are comfortable with both feet pointing out straight or with a slight external rotation. Standing on a rug is best for beginners.
2. Begin to move forward with eyes closed. Then back.
3. Align the breath with your movement and then let it go and flow.
4. Focus your full attention on the bottom of the feet. Take a few breaths.
5. Now begin to place your attention on your ankles. How do they feel/ How do they move? Take a few more breaths and just notice what you notice.
6. Now place your attention on the knees. How do they feel/ How do they move? Take a few more breaths and notice the circular motion, slightly down and around to the back and up. Stay with this for one or two minutes.
7. Now put your attention on the pelvis and imagine if you had a pencil coming out of the pelvis at a horizontal line that you would be drawing little circles. As the pelvis relaxes forward, move your body weight to the toes and then back your sacrum which allows wave like movements to flow up your spine. Feel a slight wave moving up the spine.

8. Relax your shoulders and take a nice full breath and begin to notice how the neck becomes involved in this motion. Allow the neck to move freely releasing tension at the occiput (base of skull). Again focus on the breathing, nice and easy.

9. Now imagine a WAVE moving from the Earth and up from your feet, and up to your crown chakra on the top of the head. Breathe and bring your attention now to the middle line of your body and tell your body to rediscover the most suitable muscles to hold you up most efficiently. This should take a few minutes. Pause for six seconds and repeat with mind fullness. Slowly, slowly from the ground up and ask your higher intelligence to make any and all adjustments, re-implementing and applying the laws of balance and motion.

10. The *I AM* Presence awareness now gives directions to the DNA of the body and your multidimensional self to shapeshift in beauty, balance and harmony.

11. Ask for the balance of the Five Elements of Earth, Fire, Water, Air and Ether. Now visualize the color associated with each chakra and with your mind pulse each one from the bottom up—red, orange, yellow, green, blue, violet and white/golden.

Music is an option but not necessary.

# APPENDIX VI

# Bija Seeds ☼ Mantra Meditation
# Free Gifts of Light/Sound/Energy
# A Heart Mantra for you

Thousands of years ago and before the written language was the repository for the richness of cultures, holy men, sages and wise men and women were always present within all groups of people. We find similarities of traditions such as between the Huna of Hawaii and tribes in Africa. People existing who had no contact with one another but who developed ideas, philosophy and names for things that were identical. The subconscious mind and its discoveries, generally attributed to Freud and Jung, were understood and appreciated by the early Shamans of many cultures.

The very rich traditions of India that gave birth to the beings like Buddha, Padmasambhava (who brought Buddhism from Tibet to India) and Shankara (founder of Vedanta) offer us insights into the nature of man as an evolving spiritual being, a diamond in the rough but still capable of unfolding the wonders and perfections of a Christ. Solving the riddle of the Sphinx, like discovering the Philosophers Stone or finding the kingdom within, is the last great mystery for man to solve. Science can put a man in space, but can we discover the space within a man that resonates with the highest ideas, ideals, unity, divinity, Self and Source or God?

This was, is and will always be sole purpose of the initiate who brings the Sacred Science of Nam, or the Word, or the Mantra to the ears of the disciple of truth, to push back the barriers to self-knowledge and discover what was always already the case. God and Man are One. Bija Seeds are gifts from the Creator filled with etheric energy to fuel one's own personal journey inward toward light, freedom, creativity, wisdom, the sacred, the Source or God. Bija is the seed sound and energy that proceeds all form. Mantras are powerful vibrations that work at the atomic level to assist human beings in the journey of being and becoming, of awakening.

The Mantra, the OM or Amen is beyond religion and/or perhaps before it. The Seed resonates with your primordial self and aligns ones body/mind/spirit with the cause of it's existence, delivering empowerments of knowledge, sensitivity, virtue and proofs of our eternal connection with one another and with the Supreme Being, Supreme Intelligence, the Omnipotent, present Omniscient One, in a most rewarding, step by step unfolding and glorious fashion.

A more complete study of the meditation process can be found in Section Two, page 22 in the Life Seed Documents found at www.LifeSeedCodes.com.

This GIFT, although valued in meditation centers for thousands of dollars, is offered as a free gift of love and light at most Life Seed and Diamond Heart events. Receive a gift that keeps on giving. Let your keen focus resonate a complete and wholesome path of fulfillment, satisfaction and wonder, Become more heart centered.

☼

When I am researching material from Bija meditation masters, there is never enough of the hard facts or the scientific explanations of what is happening when you enter the zone of mantra and meditation. And actually, from my own experience things have happened to me in the silence—in the field of awareness that transcends words. If someone tells you that you are not your mind, that's nice. But it does not mean anything. There is a wonderful book called <u>The Impersonal Life</u>, and, in it, the author makes this brilliant case:

*"You are not who you think you are". If that is the case then, "Who am I?"*

We are not going to tackle those big questions here but rather, take you on a little journey about the history and utilization of Bija Seed mantras. The oral tradition of the ancient world was preserved in psalm, poems, story, myth, song and dance. Memorization was a key, since reading has really only been necessary, or become a part of many cultures in the last five hundred or so years. The master or the teacher radiated such a profound energy, that there was never any questioning of the teaching or instructions. The eastern mind has simply developed in ways that the western person cannot fathom. It would be perhaps the exact opposite of taking a laptop into the Amazon and sharing this with the natives. I am sure many a native would simply say, "Who needs it, can't eat it".

But if one considers themselves to be an evolving being in an evolving universe, then certainly we must take a look at what it is we are all about, what the world is all about and what the resources are—both internal and external—that are required to succeed in meeting our goals. Sound is a building block of creation. Nothing is neutral. Everything vibrates. Westinghouse has proven that glass is not solid but is rather a slow moving liquid. Glass that sits around long enough will thicken at the bottom if laid out vertically.

Sound and vibration determine quality and character of matter. Sound and vibration can affect the consciousness of an individual and allow for positive or negative expressions. Conquering the mind and its many facets and functionalities, has been the soul function and purpose behind Yoga. The many, great yoga books and scriptures are as rich as the Bible or the Tao Te Ching of Ancient China. Great truths compliment each other.

Concerning meditation, Jesus said *"Pray in the closet and speak to the Father in private"* and *"When your eye then becomes single, your whole body will be full of light"*.

Follow any way inside, and let your flowering awareness discover the truths and realities within.

The Bija Seed Mantras are just one way to utilize meditation technology that has been a part of a very highly spiritually advanced group of people. We prefer to use as many tools and varieties of mantra, affirmations, visualization and contemplations as possible.

## APPENDIX VII

# FORM: What Diamond Heart Energy Activations *Are NOT*

What is clear to me after the practice of energy work and meditation for many years is that one is constantly in a more focused state of self-discovery and creativity. It is important in considering participating in the research and guided meditations that one understands what these activations are **NOT**.

1. This is not a form of therapy, or hypnosis of any kind or persuasion.

2. This is not a religious belief program.

3. This is not the practice of medicine, diagnosis or mental health assessment.

4. There are no beliefs required outside a normal trust that one is connected to a universal power that created us and maintains us, and that we are connected to this source of power through grace. Your sovereignty is held as a sacred trust.

5. Participants are free <u>to stop this inquiry</u> at any time either during the session or after any session. Participation is totally voluntary. Each session is scheduled as desired.

6. There are NO suggestions or advice given concerning one's way of living, one's relationships and affiliations in any way that may be considered directives.

7. There is never any recruiting to join any organization, group or congregation.

## What Diamond Heart Energy Activations Are

**What DHEA is**, is the free use of our God-given attention and inquiry unsupported by any means mechanical, electrical, chemical into our own body/mind/spirit for the sole purpose of expanding our awareness and appreciation for the gifts <u>within</u> both activated and utilized, and those we wish to awaken from a latent state. Also upon discovery we acknowledge the free right of participants to share freely any and all of the discoveries obtained within in any way that the individual may so choose. No secret hand shakes.

***The Diamond Heart Energy Activations are quantum energy conversations that honor the giver and the receiver as equal partners in a journey of self-exploration.*** These sessions encourage a new and mature way of human interaction that acknowledges the sovereignty of each individual, his or her right to choose, and to make discovery that will enhance the human experience by directly ***bringing in more quantum, electro-magnetic energy***.

It is therefore the responsibility of participants to determine if this were the appropriate time for such an adventure and to consider personally all things appropriate to such an exercise. The <u>one absolute</u> is to rest easy for a few hours afterwards and to consume sufficient plus amounts of water. (Rest easy means to lie down for at <u>least one hour)</u>

I have read the statement and freely subscribe my signature.

Name: _____ Date: _____

# Meet the Author

Rev. Brian T Roberts

I have been trying to remain as anonymous as possible here in the process of releasing the Diamond Heart Energy Activations. I became a massage therapist in 1976 and at a seminar I was taking years later our instructor told us to learn to meditate because we would be working on a lot of sick people and would need to "stay clear". I got involved with Hakomi work, a form of Body Centered Psychotherapy for a few years doing training in this work. I came from a harsh background and took a significant amount of physical abuse growing up. All of the systems of mind-body-spirit integration that I explored professionally were first and foremost for myself, for my own healing. I had incredible teachers and really kept after it for many years. I graduated from the seminary of the Church of Ageless Wisdom and was exposed to great teachings and amazing people.

I was a movement enthusiast and studied and taught the Flomotion movement awareness system for four years. I trained in a system of Hypnotherapy for one year and received sessions weekly. It took me about twenty years to ground myself in meditation. Nowadays there are many more support systems to help us. In the process of trying to find the right meditation teacher and system, I encountered many Yogi's, Christian mystics, Buddhist Lamas, Hakomi folk, Sufi's, channels, mediums, Transcendental Meditation instructors, dowsers, and many current day quantum energy systems people. All of it was and is a part of my knowledge and experience base. I practiced Alpha Brain Body balancing for ten years and during that time I performed 1000 ceremonies, weddings, christenings, and meditation initiations. For many years I woke up at 4 a.m. to meditate. I can not do this right now because I need to be more active in the world.

I truly wish I could have shared most all of these things with friends and family. Perhaps some will join me in the Diamond Heart. The meditation on the *heart mantra* at the conclusion of the 12 minute (Track 2) meditation truly helps center me. It is softly wonderful and powerful.

The Diamond Heart Energy Activations honor spirit and our connection with our own *I AM* Presence. It was built from the Unity platform and is about Oneness, plain and simple.

No cults, no guru's, no hooks, no secret hand shakes, just Presence.

Falling/Rising into a relationship with our True Self or "*I AM*" demands that we follow our hearts. *Be As You Are* because you are a star. Be inspired by everyone you can be inspired by. Kahil Gibran said in the book <u>The Prophet</u> to never put your heart into anyone's hands for only the hand of Life can contain your heart. I personally left a lot of guru's because they all had their own agendas.

Listen to the sound of the mantras and read the poems and meditations in the book and you will know enough about the author. My work with organizing the CD's and the book are done. Now I AM starting a new journey to meet my Self in all the Selves I meet on the journey, in light and mutual respect. We are here to learn the lesson of togetherness.

Let's get it done.

Namáste

Brian T Roberts

Minister of Light And Sound

## TO FULLY EXPERIENCE
### the twelve Diamond Heart activations, listen to the free audio recordings of the meditations

Note that sound vibration is one of the strongest ways to trigger activations so it is recommended to use this workbook as a secondary support to listening to the mp3's.

### To get your
### FREE Diamond Heart MP3's

Email:

lifeseedcodes108@hotmail.com
Subject Line: Send Meditations

# Complementary Clearing and Balancing

Receive your **complementary** Diamond Life Heart Weaving clearing and balancing from Brian Roberts by contacting Brian through www.LifeSeedCodes.com.

Also be sure to visit **www.LifeSeedCodes.com** for

- *Free Music Downloads*
- *Information on Diamond Heart Energy Activations*
- *One-on-One LifeSeed Sessions and free LifeSeed downloads*
- *Dowsing/Counseling Work using the LifeWeaving Process*
- *Meditation Initiation*
- *Free Remote Energy Healing Session*
- *Bodywork Services*

More information about the LifeWeaving Clearing method can be found at www.AyniLifeWeaving.com.

Namáste,

Brian

## *Namáste*

Brian welcomes your comments and encourages discussion about the Diamond Heart material and would be pleased to have you leave a book review and share your feelings.

Connect with Brian through the contact page at www.LifeseedCodes.com

www.ingramcontent.com/pod-product-compliance
Lightning Source LLC
Chambersburg PA
CBHW080346170426
43194CB00014B/2703